365 Days
with the
Saints

A YEAR OF WISDOM
FROM THE SAINTS

by

CAROL KELLY-GANGI

*This book is dedicated with love to my mother
Gwen Kelly, and in loving memory of
my father, Howard Kelly—thank you both for
a lifetime of love, prayers, and eternal support.*

Acknowledgments
I would like to gratefully thank all those whose
encouragement, suggestions, and expertise made it
possible for me to complete this book: Gwen Kelly,
Marianne Kelly, Theresa Kelly, Barbara Kelly-Vergona,
Paul and Vivian Gangi, Beverly Lindh, Annie Silvestro,
Jason Chappell, and Michelle Faulkner. And as always,
loving thanks to my husband John and to our children
John and Emily—I am so blessed in all of you.

P R E S S

an imprint of Quarto Publishing Group USA Inc.
142 West 36th Street, 4th Floor
New York, New York 10018

WELLFLEET PRESS and the distinctive Wellfleet Press logo
are trademarks of
Quarto Publishing Group USA Inc.

ISBN-13: 978-1-57715-119-7

Printed in China

2 4 6 8 10 9 7 5 3 1

www.quartous.com

IMAGE CREDITS

Alamy: © Niday Picture Library: 53; **British Library:** 71;
Getty Images: © Borgas/ullstein bild: 156; © William Thomas Cain/Hulton Archive: 43;
© DeAgostini: 14, 172, 280; © Grzegorz Galazka\Mondadori Portfolio: 219;
© ullstein bild: 161; **Metropolitan Museum of Art:** 123, 255; **National Gallery of Art**
ii, 36, 81, 165, 275; **Rijksmuseum:** viii, 18, 203, 226, 247; **Shutterstock:**
© Zvonimir Atletic: 178; © Everett Historical: 4; © FineArtImages: 258; © Jurand: 24;
© Bill Perry: 213; © Renata Sedmakova: 199, 244; © tipograffias: 262; © Patrick Wang:
240; **Superstock:** © FineArtImages: 258; **Wellcome Library,** London: 84; **Courtesy**
Wikimedia Foundation: 115, 148; Museo Nacional del Prado: 260; **National Gallery:**
21; Santa Maria del Popolo, Rome: 16; **Yale University Art Gallery:** 115

Contents

INTRODUCTION

Those from whom I receive the greatest consolations and encouragement are those whom I know to be dwelling in Paradise.

—*St. Teresa of Avila*

The saints have been a source of inspiration and guidance for Christians for centuries. This book invites readers to embark on a one-year journey with the saints—reading selections of their wisdom, a prayer, a Gospel excerpt, or a reflection for every day of the year. There is a saint featured on each day except for the days on the Roman Liturgical Calendar that are devoted to a liturgical celebration of a higher rank such as a solemnity—for example, the Assumption of Mary. For every saint, there is also a brief biographical sketch which gives some insight into the life of the saint and his or her path to holiness.

A word about why saints are remembered on specific dates. What may be surprising to some is that each day of the year has many different saints associated with it. The feast day of a saint can be the date of his or her death or the date of his or her canonization. Some saints have obligatory memorials on the Calendar; some have optional memorials; and some have been removed from the Calendar but are still venerated by the faithful and prayed to for their protection and patronage. Who are the saints included within these pages? The Blessed Virgin is known as the first disciple of Christ and is the greatest of all the saints. The Virgin Mary is richly represented in this book, not only on her solemnities and feast days, but in many excerpts from a wealth of saints who have venerated her from the earliest days of Christianity. Of course, the towering figures from our faith are here—the Apostles; the early Fathers of the Church; the Doctors of the Church; and the saints who are universally revered and beloved. Here, too, are saints who have been canonized recently such as the monumental figures of Saint Pope John Paul II and Saint Pope John XXIII. And there are saints who may be less familiar to readers but whose diverse narratives lend support to the familiar notion that God doesn't call the qualified; He qualifies the called. There is St. Josephine Bakhita, an African-American slave who found her way to freedom and to sainthood; St. Kateri Tekakwitha, an Algonquin-Mohawk saint; St. Edith Stein, a nun and convert from Judaism who was killed at Auschwitz during World War II; and St. Faustina, the Polish saint whose visions formed the basis of the cult of the Divine Mercy. While the majority of men and women within these pages are canonized saints, there are also some who are beatified and known as Blessed. Blessed Teresa of Calcutta is of course included.

The words of the saints form the heart of this book. The excerpts are as rich and varied as the saints themselves. They range from sophisticated spiritual insights; to the spare eloquence of deathbed whispers; to the impassioned words of forgiveness from saints facing martyrdom. Some universal themes that emerge from the selections are an unending love for God and for all of humankind; a fervent desire to spread the Good News of Jesus Christ; and deep devotion to the Blessed Mother. In some excerpts, one saint recalls another saint—weaving a rich tapestry of insights from one saint to another. St. Teresa of Avila relates her first impressions of St. John of the Cross. St. Augustine reveals how St. John the Baptist bridges the Old and New Testaments. Saint Pope John Paul II explains why St. Faustina is a saint for the new millennium.

It is sincerely hoped that within these pages, you will find something to help you on your own spiritual journey. May the words of the saints reveal a small measure of their holiness and humanity; to inspire, challenge, and guide us as we continue on our own path to sanctity.

—*Carol Kelly-Gangi*
Rumson, New Jersey, 2015

JANUARY

....

THE SOLEMNITY OF
THE BLESSED VIRGIN MARY,
THE MOTHER OF GOD

My soul proclaims the greatness of the Lord; my spirit rejoices in God my savior. For he has looked upon his handmaid's lowliness; behold, from now on will all ages call me blessed. The Mighty One has done great things for me, and holy is his name. His mercy is from age to age to those who fear him. He has shown might with his arm, dispersed the arrogant of mind and heart. He has thrown down the rulers from their thrones but lifted up the lowly. The hungry he has filled with good things; the rich he has sent away empty. He has helped Israel his servant, remembering his mercy, according to his promise to our fathers, to Abraham and to his descendants forever.

—Luke 1:46–55

This woman of faith, Mary of Nazareth, the Mother of God, has been given to us as a model in our pilgrimage of faith. From Mary we learn to surrender to God's will in all things. From Mary, we learn to trust even when all hope seems gone. From Mary, we learn to love Christ, her Son and the Son of God. For Mary is not only the Mother of God, she is the Mother of the Church as well.

—Pope John Paul II

OPPOSITE: The Blessed Virgin Mary

SAINT BASIL THE GREAT

(329–379) Bishop and Doctor of the Church

There is still time for endurance, time for patience, time for healing, time for change. Have you slipped? Rise up. Have you sinned? Cease. Do not stand among sinners, but leap aside.

—St. Basil the Great

SAINT GREGORY NAZIANZEN

(329–390) Bishop and Doctor of the Church

Give something, however small, to the one in need. For it is not small to one who has nothing. Neither is it small to God, if we have given what we could.

—St. Gregory Nazianzen

JANUARY 3

SAINT GENEVIEVE

(422–512) The Patroness of Paris and virgin, she led a life of prayer, faith, and charity. She dedicated herself to Christ at the age of seven.

Blessed be you, my Father. What you ask of me is the most cherished desire of my heart. I ask only that by your prayers Our Lord will accomplish my desire.

—St. Genevieve's response to St. Germanus of Auxerre who
asked her if she wished to consecrate herself to the Lord

SAINT ELIZABETH ANN SETON

(1774–1821) Born to a wealthy Episcopalian family in New York, St. Elizabeth married William Seton and had five children. After her husband died, she was left to raise five young children on her own. Finding herself drawn to the Catholic faith for some time, she finally converted in 1805. In 1808, she founded the first Catholic school in Baltimore, and founded the Sisters of Charity, the first American religious community for women, the following year. Mother Seton became the first American-born citizen to be beatified in 1963 and canonized in 1975.

Oh, that my Soul could go up with my blessed Lord! That it might be where He is also—Thy Will be done—my time is in Thy hands. O, my Savior, while the pilgrimage of this life must still go on to fulfill Thy gracious purpose let the Spirit of my mind follow Thee to Thy mansions of glory. To Thee alone it belongs, receive it in mercy, perfect it in truth, and preserve it upspotted from the world.

—St. Elizabeth Ann Seton

SAINT ANGELA OF FOLIGNO

(1248–1309) Founder, Christian mystic, and writer. She was beatified in 1701 and canonized on October 9, 2013 by Pope Francis pursuant to the doctrine of "equivalent canonization," wherein the usual judicial process is waived and the blessed's liturgical cult is extended to the worldwide church.

No one can be saved without divine light. Divine light causes us to begin and to make progress, and it leads us to the summit of perfection. Therefore if you want to begin and to receive this divine light, pray. If you have begun to make progress and want this light to be intensified within you, pray. And if you have reached the summit of perfection, and want to be super-illumined so as to remain in that state, pray.

—St. Angela of Foligno

SAINT JOHN NEUMANN

(1811–1860) Born in the present day Czech Republic, St. John journeyed to the United States to do missionary work and was ordained in New York in 1836. In 1840 he entered the Redemptorists, and did missionary work in Maryland, Virginia, and Ohio. In 1852, he was named Bishop of Philadelphia and worked tirelessly to establish Catholic schools and parishes. Known for his sanctity and great intellect, he was the first American bishop to be beatified (1963) and he was canonized in 1977.

My God, how great Thou art, how wonderful in all Thy works! Teach me Thy will that I may begin and end all my actions for Thy greater glory. Speak to me, Oh my God, let me know Thy will, for behold I am ready to fulfill Thy every command. The difficult, the irksome, I will patiently endure for love of Thee.

Oh my God, I thank Thee for the love Thou hast planted in my heart. I will cultivate this precious flower. I will guard it night and day that nothing may injure it. Do Thou, Oh Lord, water it with the dew of Thy grace.

—Prayers found in Bishop Neumann's diary

THE EPIPHANY OF THE LORD

If the Magi had come in search of an earthly King, they would have been disconcerted at finding that they had taken the trouble to come such a long way for nothing. Consequently they would have neither adored nor offered gifts. But since they sought a heavenly King, though they found in Him no signs of royal pre-eminence, yet, content with the testimony of the star alone, they adored: for they saw a man, and they acknowledged a God.

—St. John Chrysostom

OPPOSITE: Elizabeth Seton

On the feast of the Epiphany, as we recall Jesus' manifestation to humanity in the face of a Child, may we sense the Magi at our side, as wise companions on the way. Their example helps us to lift our gaze towards the star and to follow the great desires of our heart.

—*Pope Francis*

....

JANUARY 7

SAINT RAYMOND OF PENYAFORT

(1175–1275) Religious, theologian, and co-founder of Order of Our Lady of Ransom. A compiler of important canon law that was codified as Church law for centuries, he is the patron saint of lawyers.

Look then on Jesus, the author and preserver of faith: in complete sinlessness he suffered, and at the hands of those who were his own, and was numbered among the wicked. As you drink the cup of the Lord Jesus (how glorious it is!), give thanks to the Lord, the giver of all blessings.

—*St. Raymond of Penyafort*

....

JANUARY 8

SAINT GUDULA

(d. 712) Religious who devoted her life to prayer, fasting, and charitable works. She is the patron saint of Brussels.

By the true love of Christ
In it you became the illustrious Bride;
Remaining a Virgin, you knew the True Joy
Of being in spirit the mother of the poor.

You vowed your holy life to the wretched
And you saw the image of the Lord in the poor;
Pray without ceasing to the Master
For us who celebrate your sacred memory with all our hearts.

In the world, you followed the same life
As consecrated nuns in the cloister;
Without vows, you fulfilled your vow:
To radiate around you the love of Christ
And, because you did this for the least of his brothers,
He received you into the light of His Kingdom;
Blessed Gudula, God-Bearer, intercede for all
Who venerate your memory.

—*from Orthodox hymn honoring St. Gudula*

....

JANUARY 9

BLESSED TOMMASO REGGIO

(1818–1901) Priest, bishop, and archbishop. Devoted to helping the poor and displaced, he was the founder of the Sisters of Saint Martha, who dedicated themselves to ministering to the poor. Known to pray every night from 3:00 to 6:00 in the morning, he was beatified by Pope John Paul 11 on September 3, 2000.

I want to become a saint, cost what it may, living my life in accordance with the two cornerstones of Christianity: prayer and ascesis.

—*Blessed Tommaso Reggio, at his ordination*

His message can be summed up in two words: truth and charity. Truth, first of all, which means attentive listening to God's word and courageous zeal in defending and spreading the teachings of the

Gospel. Then charity, which spurs people to love God and, for love of him, to embrace everyone since they are brothers and sisters in Christ. If there was a preference in Tommaso Reggio's choices, it was for those who found themselves in hardship and suffering.

—from homily of Pope John Paul II at the beatification of Blessed Tommaso

. . . .

JANUARY 10

SAINT WILLIAM OF BOURGES

(c. 1147–1209) Religious who became the Archbishop of Bourges. He lived a life of great prayer and austerity. He is said to have died while on his knees in prayer on January 10, 1209.

He wore coarse clothes, never ate any meat, and attended to his parishioners in sincerity—stating that his mission was to assist those poor in body and spirit. . . . He was a man who defended the poor, protected the rights of those less fortunate, and lived causing no harm to any being. His life was one of gentleness and compassion toward all.

—Holly H. Roberts, Vegetarian Christian Saints

. . . .

JANUARY 11

SAINT FRANCISCA SALESIA AVIAT

(1844–1914) Religious and co-founder of Sister Oblates of Francis de Sales, dedicated to ministering to young working-class girls, for whom she opened many schools and homes. She was canonized on November 25, 2001 by Pope John Paul II.

Let us establish a permanent Spring season in our heart through "yes" often repeated to all of God's permissions and wills.

—St. Francisca Salesia Aviat

. . . .

JANUARY 12

SAINT MARGUERITE BOURGEOYS

(1620–1700) Religious and founder of the Sisters of the Congregation of Notre-Dame of Montreal, devoted to teaching children in Montreal. Canonized by Pope John Paul II in 1982, she became the first female Catholic saint in Canada.

It seems to me that we do not pay enough attention to prayer, for unless it arises from the heart which ought to be the center, it is no more than a fruitless dream. Prayer ought to carry over into our words, our thoughts and our actions. We must strive as much as we can to reflect on what we ask or promise. We do not do this if we do not pay attention to our prayers.

—St. Marguerite Bourgeoys

. . . .

JANUARY 13

SAINT HILARY OF POITIERS

(c. 315–368) Theologian, bishop, and Doctor of the Church

He by whom man was made had nothing to gain by becoming man; it was our gain that God was incarnate and dwelt among us, making all flesh his home by taking upon him the flesh of one. We were raised because he was lowered; shame to him was glory to us. He, being God, made flesh his residence, and we in return are lifted anew from the flesh to God.

—St. Hilary of Poitiers

BLESSED PETER DONDERS

(1807–1887) Priest and missionary who ministered to Africans, native peoples, and lepers for more than forty years.

If only, by sacrificing my own life, I could bring all people to know and love God as he deserves. But let God's holy will be done in all things. The Holy Will of God and perfect obedience in all things have always been my consolation, and I hope that it may still be so at the hour of my death. Amen.

—*Blessed Peter Donders*

SAINT ARNOLD JANSSEN

(1837–1909) Priest and founder of the Society of the Divine Word and the Servant Sisters of the Holy Ghost, both devoted to missionary work. He was canonized by Pope John Paul II in October of 2003.

In spring we see how the plants, beautifully formed, sprout from the dark, dirty soil and soon stand before us in all their colorful beauty and with sparkling, affectionate eyes gaze at us like messengers from God. Where do they come from? The finger of God, the Holy Spirit, is at work here.

—*St. Arnold Janssen*

SAINT BERARD AND COMPANIONS

(died c. 1226) Saints Berard, Peter, Accursius, Adjutus, and Otto were Franciscan friars sent by St. Francis to preach to the Moors. While in Morocco, they were executed by the sultan who was displeased by their preaching. This tragedy inspired the young St. Anthony of Padua to join the Franciscans.

Have no fear of being thought insignificant or unbalanced, but preach repentance with courage and simplicity. Have faith in the Lord, who has overcome the world. His spirit speaks in you and through you, calling men and women to turn to Him and observe His precepts.

—St. Francis quoted in The Legend of the Three Companions

. . . .

JANUARY 17

SAINT ANTHONY THE GREAT

(251–356) Known as the Father of Christian Monasticism, he lived as a hermit and devoted himself to a life of prayer, silence, and labor. In 305 he founded a monastery.

Our life and our death is with our neighbor. If we gain our brother, we have gained God, but if we scandalize our brother, we have sinned against Christ.

—St. Anthony the Great

. . . .

JANUARY 18

SAINT VINCENZA MARY LOPEZ Y VICUNA

(1847–1890) Born to wealthy parents, she refused an arranged marriage and took a vow of chastity. She was the founder of Daughters of Mary Immaculate, devoted to helping poor women working as domestic servants.

I count myself happier in the service of these my sisters, than the great ones of this world in the service of their lords and kings.

—St. Vincenza Mary Lopez y Vicuna

SAINT FILLAN

(died c. 288) Abbot and hermit who lived in Scotland. He is said to have drank from and blessed a stream that thereafter had healing powers, especially for those suffering from mental illness.

Thence to St. Fillan's blessed well,
Whose spring can frenzied dreams dispel,
And the crazed brain restore

—*from first canto of* Marmion *by Sir Walter Scott*

SAINT SEBASTIAN

(died c. 288) Roman soldier who was martyred for his faith. He is the patron saint of athletes.

St. Sebastian,
You chose to be a Soldier of Christ
and dared to spread faith in Him, the King of Kings.
Protect all athletes from injury and harm,
and pray for us to have
the endurance to pursue our heavenly prize: eternal life
with Christ. Amen.

—*Prayer to St. Sebastian*

....

JANUARY 21

SAINT AGNES

(died c. 304) St. Agnes was martyred at the age thirteen for refusing to marry any suitor because she had consecrated herself to Christ. Renowned for her heroism, she is one of the most revered Roman martyrs.

All nations, especially their Christian communities, praise in word and writing the life of St. Agnes. She triumphed over her tender age as well as over the merciless tyrant. To the crown of spotless innocence she added the glory of martyrdom.

—*St. Jerome writing about St. Agnes*

....

JANUARY 22

SAINT VINCENT PALLOTTI

(1795–1850) Priest and founder of Society of the Catholic Apostolate. He spent his life ministering to the poor and needy. He was canonized in 1963 by Pope John XXIII.

Remember that the Christian life is one of action; not of speech and daydreams. Let there be few words and many deeds, and let them be done well.

—*St. Vincent Pallotti*

....

JANUARY 23

BLESSED HENRY SUSO

(c. 1300–1366) Dominican friar, mystic, spiritual writer and advisor. He was beatified in 1831.

Worldly people often purchase Hell at a very dear price by sacrificing themselves to please the world.

—Blessed Henry Suso

······················

JANUARY 24

SAINT FRANCIS DE SALES

(1567–1622) Bishop, scholar, spiritual writer, co-founder of the Order of the Visitation, and Doctor of the Church. He is known for his great sanctity and gentleness.

Try interrupting the meditations of someone who is very attached to her spiritual exercises and you will see her upset, flustered, taken aback. A person who has this true freedom will leave her prayer, unruffled, gracious toward the person who has unexpectedly disturbed her, for to her it's all the same—serving God by meditating or serving Him by responding to her neighbor. Both are the will of God, but helping the neighbor is necessary at that particular moment.

—St. Francis de Sales

······················

JANUARY 25

CONVERSION OF SAINT PAUL THE APOSTLE

(c. 5–c. 67) Apostle and martyr. A religious fanatic against the early Church, he was en route to Damascus to arrest Christians when he experienced a dramatic conversion to Christianity and became an Apostle. His writings have had a profound impact on the development of Christianity.

OPPOSITE: Saint Agnes

Love is patient, love is kind. It is not jealous, {love} is not pompous, it is not inflated, it is not rude, it does not seek its own interests, it is not quick-tempered, it does not brood over injury, it does not rejoice over wrongdoing but rejoices with the truth. It bears all things, believes all things, hopes all things, endures all things. (1 Corinthinans 13:4-7)

You cannot be a conscious Christian without St. Paul. He translated the teachings of Christ into a doctrinal structure that, even with the additions of a vast number of thinkers, theologians and pastors, has resisted and still exists after two thousand years.

—*Pope Franis*

. . . .

JANUARY 26

SAINT TIMOTHY

(died c. 97) Bishop. St. Timothy was a faithful friend of St. Paul and beloved by his fellow disciple with whom he worked closely for fifteen years. St. Paul sent St. Timothy on many difficult missions; he was martyred in or around the year 97.

I remind you to stir into flame the gift of God that you have through the imposition of my hands. For God did not give us a spirit of cowardice but rather of power and love and self-control. So do not be ashamed of your testimony to our Lord, nor of me, a prisoner for his sake; but bear your share of hardship for the gospel with the strength that comes from God.

—*St. Paul's Second Letter to Timothy 1:6–8*

OPPOSITE: Conversion of Saint Paul the Apostle

DE
H: TIMOTHEVS
op Ziender der
Kerken van
Aziën,

Te Efefen, van de Heydenen wreedelyk omgebragt.

TIMOTHEUS, die 't eerst tot Bisschop aangesteld
Van Efezen, daar als een Euangely-held
De kerk opbouwd, ten trots Dianaas naam en Tempel;
Drukt met zyn bloed op haar Gods merk en zegel-stempel.

SAINT TITUS

(died c. 94) Bishop. St. Titus was a close friend and valued disciple of St. Paul. He worked tirelessly as the Bishop of Crete and spread the faith until he died of natural causes in his nineties.

For the grace of God has appeared, saving all and training us to reject godless ways and worldly desires and to live temperately, justly, and devoutly in this age, as we await the blessed hope, the appearance of the glory of the great God and of our savior Jesus Christ, who gave himself for us to deliver us from all lawlessness and to cleanse for himself a people as his own, eager to do what is good.

—*St. Paul's Letter to Titus 2:11–14*

. . . .

JANUARY 27

SAINT ANGELA MERICI

(c. 1474–1540) Religious who established schools for the instruction of young girls and founded the Ursulines at Brescia, the first teaching order of women in the Church.

My last word to you is that you live in harmony, united together, all of one heart and one will. Be bound to one another by the bond of charity, esteeming one another, helping one another, bearing with one another in Jesus Christ.

—*St. Angela Merci*

OPPOSITE: Saint Timothy

SAINT THOMAS AQUINAS

(1225–1274) Priest, prolific theologian, teacher, Doctor of the Church, and Angelic Doctor

If, then, you are looking for the way by which you should go, take Christ, because He Himself is the way.

—*St. Thomas Aquinas*

ST. GILDAS THE WISE

(c. 500–570) Abott, teacher, and founder. He is well known for writing a history of British vice and is thus known as the first British historian.

For our Lord Jesus Christ had given him such gifts of healings that, through his prayers, the blind received their sight, their hearing was restored to the deaf, and their power to walk to the lame and the maimed; the demoniacs were cured, the lepers were cleansed, and all the sick were healed. St. Gildas, therefore, continued in the preaching of the Gospel of Christ, teaching the true faith through all the provinces, and converted his nation to the true and catholic faith.

—*from* Two Lives of Gildas *by a monk of Ruys and Caradoc of Llanfaran*

OPPOSITE: Saint Thomas Aquinas

SAINT HYACINTHA MARISCOTTI

(1585–1640) St. Hyacintha entered a Franciscan convent but lived frivolously for years there until illness brought about her conversion. Thereafter, she lived a life of charity and devotion to her faith.

The sort of people who most appeal to me are those who are despised, who are devoid of self love and who have little sensible consolation. . . . The cross, to suffer, to persevere bravely in spite of the lack of all sweetness and relish in prayer: This is the true sign of the spirit of God.

—*St. Hyacintha Mariscotti*

SAINT JOHN BOSCO

(1815–1888) Priest, teacher, and founder of the Salesian Society of St. Francis de Sales and the Daughters of Mary Help of Christians.

The true Christian should be willing to endure the sufferings of the spirit as Jesus Christ did when He was betrayed by one of His disciples, denied by another, and abandoned by all.

—*St. John Bosco*

FEBRUARY

FEBRUARY 1

SAINT BRIGID OF IRELAND

(c. 451–525) Founder. St. Brigid is the founder of the first convent in Ireland and founder and abbess of a double monastery at Kildare. She is known for her life of charity, compassion, and joyful spirituality. A key figure in the early Irish Church, she is the co-patroness of Ireland along with Sts. Patrick and Columba, with whom she is buried.

I would like an abundance of peace. I would like full vessels of charity. I would like rich treasures of mercy. I would like cheerfulness to preside over all.

—*St. Brigid of Ireland*

....

FEBRUARY 2

FEAST OF THE PRESENTATION OF THE LORD

Now there was a man in Jerusalem whose name was Simeon. This man was righteous and devout, awaiting the consolation of Israel, and the holy Spirit was upon him. It had been revealed to him by the holy Spirit that he should not see death before he had seen the Messiah of the Lord. He came in the Spirit into the temple; and when the parents brought in the child Jesus to perform the custom of the law in regard to him, he took him into his arms and blessed God, saying:

"Now, Master, you may let your servant go in peace, according to your word, for my eyes have seen your salvation, which you prepared in sight of all the peoples, a light for revelation to the Gentiles, and glory for your people Israel."

The child's father and mother were amazed at what was said about him; and Simeon blessed them and said to Mary his mother, "Behold, this child is destined for the fall and rise of many in Israel, and to be a sign that will be contradicted (and you yourself a sword will pierce) so that the thoughts of many hearts may be revealed."

—*Luke 2:29–36*

SAINT BLAISE

(died c. 316) Bishop. St. Blaise was the bishop of Sebaste in Armenia who was martyred in the early fourth century. It is believed that on his way to prison, he encountered a mother whose child had a severe throat ailment. She begged for him to help and St. Blaise cured the child. During the blessing of throats, the priest holds two candles in the form of a cross at each person's throat and prays the following blessing:

Through the intercession of St. Blaise, bishop and martyr, may God deliver you from every disease of the throat, and from every other illness. In the name of the Father, and of the Son, and of the Holy Spirit.

—*Blessing of St. Blaise*

SAINT JOAN OF VALOIS

(1464–1505) Religious and founder. She was the daughter of Louis XI, King of France. After twenty years of a forced marriage to the Duke of Orleans, she founded the Sisters of the Annunciation of the Blessed Virgin Mary and devoted her life to prayer and charitable works.

OPPOSITE: Saint Brigid of Ireland

God be praised who has allowed this, that I may serve Him better than I have heretofore done.

—*St. Joan of Valois, at the dissolution of her marriage*

SAINT AGATHA

(died c. 251) Virgin and martyr. As a girl, St. Agatha consecrated herself to Christ. She was cruelly tortured and martyred for her refusal to give herself to a Roman senator. She is the patron saint of nurses.

Dear Virgin and Martyr, whom the Church recalls in her liturgy, you heroically resisted the temptation of a degenerate ruler. Subjected to long and horrible tortures, you remained faithful to your heavenly Spouse. St. Peter, we are told, gave you some solace, and so you are invoked by nurses. Encourage them to see Christ in the sick and to render true service to them. Amen.

—*A Nurse's Prayer to St. Agatha*

MEMORIAL OF SAINT PAUL MIKI AND COMPANIONS

(d. 1597) Martyrs. St. Paul Miki and his twenty-five companions were crucified by the Japanese authorities after rumors circulated that they were conspiring with the French and Portuguese to overthrow Japan. The martyred group included priests, catechists, and Japanese lay Christians, including altar boys. St. Paul Miki was a Jesuit novice who heroically preached his last sermon from the cross.

The sentence of judgment says these men came to Japan from the Philippines, but I did not come from any other country. I am a true Japanese. The only reason for my being killed is that I have taught the doctrine of Christ. I certainly did teach the doctrine of Christ. I thank God it is for this reason I die. I believe that I am telling only the truth before I die. I know you believe me and I want to say to you all once again: Ask Christ to help you to become happy. I obey Christ. After Christ's example I forgive my persecutors. I do not hate them. I ask God to have pity on all, and I hope my blood will fall on my fellow men as a fruitful rain.

—*St. Paul Miki's words from the cross*

. . . .

FEBRUARY 7

BLESSED PIUS IX

(1792–1878) Pope. Blessed Pope Pius IX was pope for thirty-two years, the longest pontificate in Church history save for St. Peter. He is responsible for the dogma of the Immaculate Conception of Mary and the dogma of papal infallibility. He was beatified on September 3, 2000.

Give me an army saying the Rosary and I will conquer the world.

—*Blessed Pope Pius IX*

. . . .

FEBRUARY 8

SAINT JOSEPHINE BAKHITA

(1869–1947) Religious. Kidnapped and sold into slavery as a child in the Sudan, St. Josephine suffered years of torture and humiliations until she found her way to Italy through a benevolent owner. In 1893, she joined the Canossian sisters and spent her life teaching and helping her community. Known for her humility, simplicity, and sweet disposition, she was canonized in October of 2000 by Pope John Paul II. She is the first saint from and the patron saint of the Sudan.

Seeing the sun, the moon and the stars, I said to myself: who could be the Master of these beautiful things? And I felt a great desire to see him, to know him and to pay him homage.

—*St. Josephine Bakhita*

FEBRUARY 9

SAINT MIGUEL FEBRES CORDERO

(1854–1910) Religious. Born to a prominent family in Ecuador, St. Miguel suffered from an unknown disability that prevented him from standing until he was five years old. He joined the Institute of the Brothers of the Christian Schools, completed his studies, and taught for thirty-two years. Known for his dedication to his students and devotion to his faith, St. Miguel was canonized in October of 1984 by Pope John Paul II.

The heart is rich when it is content, and the heart is always content when its desires are focused on God. Nothing can bring one greater happiness than doing God's will.

—*St. Miguel Febres Cordero*

FEBRUARY 10

SAINT SCHOLASTICA

(c. 480–543) Founder. The twin sister of St. Benedict, St. Scholastica is the founder of the Order of Benedictine nuns only miles away from the monastery founded by her brother. The siblings would visit once a year where they would pray and converse together.

Please do not leave me tonight; let us go on until morning talking about the delights of the spiritual life.

—*St. Scholastica, spoken to her brother St. Benedict several days before her death*

. . . .

FEBRUARY 11

APPARITION OF THE BLESSED VIRGIN MARY AT LOURDES

The Blessed Virgin Mary appeared to young Bernadette Soubirous at Lourdes in France on February 11, 1858. Our Lady would appear a total of eighteen times to Bernadette.

I am the Immaculate Conception.

—*Our Lady of Lourde's response to Bernadette when she asked the beautiful lady her name, March 25, 1858*

O my Mother, it is to your heart that I come to lay down the anguish of my heart; it is there that I draw strength and courage.

—*St. Bernadette Soubirous*

. . . .

FEBRUARY 12

SAINT SATURNINUS AND COMPANIONS

(died c. 304) Priest and lay people. During the rule of Diocletian in a Roman province of Africa, a group of forty-nine early Christians, including St. Saturninus, who was the presiding priest, his family, and others were arrested, tried, tortured, and martyred for failing to hand over the sacred scripture to be burned.

O God, who did inflame the hearts of your sainted Martyrs with an admirable zeal for the salvation of souls, grant us, we beseech You, what we now ask that you hear our intentions, so that the favors obtained through their intercession may make manifest before men the power and glory of Your name. Amen.

SAINT CATHERINE DE RICCI

(1522–1590) Religious. A Dominican nun well known for her mystical meditations on the suffering of Christ called the "Ecstasy of the Passion" which she experienced weekly for a period of twelve years.

O Blessed St. Catherine de Ricci, you who experienced the Passion of Christ through your mystical union in His suffering, pray for us that we may take up our own Cross daily, and join our pain and suffering to that which Jesus endured. For it is only through the suffering of the Cross that we may rejoice in the glory of the resurrection. We ask this through our Lord, Jesus Christ, our Merciful Savior who lives and reigns with the Father and the Holy Spirit, one God, forever and ever. Amen.

SAINT VALENTINE

(died c. 270) Several early martyrs are remembered on this day. One of them was a priest who was martyred for his faith during the reign of Emperor Claudius II in the third century. From the late middle ages, St. Valentine has been associated with courtly love. He is the patron saint of love and happy marriages.

Too late have I loved you, O Beauty so ancient and so new, too late have I loved you! You were with me, but I was not with you. You cried out and pierced my deafness. You enlightened my blindness. I tasted you and I am hungry for you. You touched me, and I am afire with longing for your embrace.

—St. Augustine of Hippo

Perfect love means putting up with people's shortcomings, feeling no surprise at their weaknesses, finding encouragement even in the slightest evidence of good qualities in them.

—St. Thérèse of Lisieux

It is always springtime in the heart that loves God.

—St. John Vianney

· · · · · · · · · · · · · ·

FEBRUARY 15

SAINT FAUSTINUS AND SAINT JOVITA

(died c. 121) Priests and martyrs. Brothers who were martyred in Brescia during the persecution of Hadrian. They are known for their zealous preaching of Christianity while the bishop of the area was said to be in hiding for fear of persecution.

The spirit of Christ is a spirit of martyrdom, at least of mortification and penance. It is always the spirit of the cross. The remains of the old man, of sin and of death, must be extinguished, before one can be made heavenly by putting on affections which are divine. What mortifies the senses and the flesh gives life to the spirit, and what weakens and subdues the body strengthens the soul.

—from Butler's Lives of the Saints, 1866

SAINT ONESIMUS

(died c. 68) Priest, bishop, and martyr. While a slave, Onesimus robbed his master and escaped to Rome. Once there, he encountered St. Paul, then a prisoner, who converted him to Christianity. St. Paul sent him back to his former master with a letter asking for pardon. Afterwards, Onesimus returned to St. Paul and became his faithful disciple.

O God, You enabled St. Onesimus to fight to the death for justice. Through his intercession enable us to bear all adversity and with all our strength hasten to You Who alone are life. Amen.

SEVEN FOUNDERS OF THE SERVITE ORDER

(thirteenth century) Founders. A group of seven noblemen from Florence who saw a vision of the Virgin Mary and were moved to form a religious community under the name of Servants of Mary or Servites and lead lives of prayer and penance.

O Lord Jesus Christ Who, in order to renew the memory of the sorrows of Thy most holy Mother, hast through the seven blessed fathers enriched Thy Church with the new Order of Servites; mercifully grant that we may be so united in their sorrows as to share in their joys. Who livest and reignest, world without end. Amen.

SAINT BERNADETTE SOUBIROUS

(1844–1879) Religious. As a girl of fourteen, St. Bernadette received eighteen apparitions of the Blessed Virgin Mary. St. Bernadette faced much illness and suffering during her religious life and she died at the age of thirty-six while reciting the Hail Mary.

Nothing is anything more to me; everything is nothing to me, but Jesus: neither things nor persons, neither ideas nor emotions, neither honor nor sufferings. Jesus is for me honor, delight, heart and soul.

—*St. Bernadette*

BLESSED ALVAREZ OF CORDOVA

(1350–1430) Religious. Dominican friar, confessor, founder, and teacher. He is traditionally thought to have set up and preached about images of Christ's Passion that formed the basis for the Stations of the Cross.

God of mercy, you endowed Blessed Alvarez with the gifts of penance and divine love. With the help of his prayers and example may we always bear the suffering of Christ in our bodies and your love in our hearts. Amen.

BLESSED JACINTA MARTO
AND FRANCISCO MARTO

(1910–1920), (1908–1919) Lay people. Two of the three children who received apparitions of Our Lady of Fatima. The Blessed Virgin asked them to pray the rosary for intentions including peace, and an end to the war being fought in Portugal, and the conversion of Russia. Both children died from the flu several years after the apparitions. Lucia, the third child, lived to become a Carmelite nun and died in 2005. Nearly twenty million people a year visit the shrine of Our Lady of Fatima.

Mary points to Jesus. She asks us to bear witness to Jesus, she constantly guides us to her son Jesus, because in him alone do we find salvation. He alone can change the water of our loneliness, difficulties and sin into the wine of encounter, joy and forgiveness. He alone.

—*Pope Francis, praying in front of the statue of Our Lady of Fatima that was sent to Rome from the shrine at Fatima, October 13, 2013*

. . . .
FEBRUARY 21
SAINT PETER DAMIAN

(1007–1072) Religious, Bishop, and Doctor of the Church. St. Peter Damian was an orphan who was severely neglected by one of his brothers as a child, but rescued by another brother who thereafter cared for him lovingly. In the course of his eighty-three years, he taught at university, became a monk, wrote many works of theology, and was later appointed bishop and cardinal. A reformer, theologian, and servant of the poor, he was declared a Doctor of the Church in 1828.

Do not be depressed. Do not let your weakness make you impatient, Instead, let the serenity of your spirit shine through your face. Let the joy of your mind burst forth. Let words of thanks break from your lips.

—*St. Peter Damian*

SAINT PETER THE APOSTLE

Apostle and first Bishop of Rome. On Vatican Hill in Rome, during the reign of Nero, Peter was crucified.

Blessed are you, Simon son of Jonah. For flesh and blood has not revealed this to you, but my heavenly Father. And so I say to you, you are Peter, and upon this rock I will build my church, and the gates of the netherworld shall not prevail against it. I will give you the keys to the kingdom of heaven. Whatever you bind on earth shall be bound in heaven; and whatever you loose on earth shall be loosed in heaven.

—Matthew 16:17–20

O Holy Apostle,
because you are the Rock
upon which Almighty God has built His church;
obtain for me I pray you,
lively faith, firm hope and burning love;
complete detachment from myself,
contempt of the world,
patience in adversity,
humility in prosperity,
recollection in prayer,
purity of heart,
a right intention in all my works,
diligence in fulfilling the duties of my state of life,
constancy in my resolutions,
resignation to the will of God
and perseverance in the grace of God even unto death;
that so, by means of your intercession

and your glorious merits,
I may be worthy to appear
before the chief and eternal Shepherd of souls,
Jesus Christ,
Who with the Father
and the Holy Spirit
lives and reigns for ever.
Amen.
—*Novena to St. Peter*

. . . .

FEBRUARY 23

SAINT POLYCARP

(died c. 155) Bishop and martyr. A disciple of St. John the Apostle, St. Polycarp was a great leader of the early Christian Church. In his eighties, he was apprehended and condemned to death for refusing to renounce Christ.

Eighty and six years have I served Him, and, He never did me any injury; how then can I blaspheme my King and my Savior.

—*St. Polycarp, refusing to renounce Jesus before his martyrdom*

. . . .

FEBRUARY 24

BLESSED TOMMASO MARIA FUSCO

(1831–1891) Priest, missionary, and founder of both the *Priestly Society of the Catholic Apostolate* to support missions, and the Daughters of Charity of the Most Precious Blood. Called by Pope John Paul II, "an example and a guide to holiness for priests."

OPPOSITE: Saint Peter the Apostle

May work and suffering for God always be your glory and in your work and suffering, may God be your consolation on this earth, and your recompense in heaven. Patience is the safeguard and pillar of all the virtues.

—*Blessed Tommaso Maria Fusco*

· · · · · · · · · · · · · ·

SAINT CAESARIUS OF NAZIANZEN

(died 369) Medical doctor. Brother of St. Gregory of Nazianzen, he completed his medical studies and became a trusted physician. He was offered bribes and favors to give up his faith but resisted. Feeling called by God, he gave away his possessions and retreated into a life of prayer.

Lord Jesus,
Divine Physician, who in your earthly life showed special concern
for those who suffer and entrusted to your disciples the ministry of
healing, make us ever ready to alleviate the trials of our brethren.
Make each one of us, aware of the great mission that is entrusted
to him, strive always to be, in the performance of daily service, an
instrument of your merciful love. Enlighten our minds, guide our
hands, make our hearts diligent and compassionate. Ensure that in
every patient we know how to discern the features of your divine Face.

—*from Pope John Paul II's Prayer of the Catholic Physician*

FEBRUARY 26

SAINT ISABEL OF FRANCE

(1224–1270) Founder. She was the daughter of King Louis VIII who consecrated herself to God and refused the hand of various noble suitors. She founded the Franciscan Monastery of the Humility of the Blessed Virgin Mary in Paris though she never became a nun. She was known for her acts of charity and service to the poor, and her cult was approved in 1521.

We beheld in her a mirror of innocence, and at the same time an admirable model of penance, a lily of purity, a fragrant rose of patience and self-renunciation, and endless fountain of goodness and mercy.

—from one of the court ladies to Princess Isabel
quoted in The Franciscan Book of Saints *edited by Marion Habig*

....

FEBRUARY 27

SAINT GABRIEL OF OUR LADY OF SORROWS

(1838–1862) Religious. St. Gabriel was a typical teenager who found something lacking in his life and was led to the religious life. He joined the Passionists and transformed his life into one of virtue. He had a special devotion to Our Lady of Sorrows. He died at twenty-four from consumption; he is the patron saint of students and young people.

By the shining example of St. Gabriel, you dear young people, draw the courage to be faithful disciples of Christ.

—Pope John Paul II

POPE SAINT HILARY

(d. 468) Religious, pope. Pope Saint Hilary was the successor to Pope Leo. He was known as wise and faithful. He rebuilt many churches, quelled disputes, and strengthened the Church during his papacy.

Pope Saint Hilary, you did much to promote unity in the Church during your lifetime and papacy. Help us to work for unity in our own lives, in our communities, in the Church, and in the world. We ask this through Jesus Christ our Lord, Amen

MARCH

MARCH 1

SAINT DAVID OF WALES

(520–589) Priest, founder, archbishop. Believed to be a descendent of King Arthur, he studied under St. Paulinus, engaged in missionary work, and founded many monasteries in Wales and England. He and his monks lived lives of strict austerity. He is the patron saint of Wales.

Be joyful, brothers and sisters. Keep your faith, and do the little things that you have seen and heard with me.

—*St. David's last words to his monks and followers*

· · · · · · · · · ·

MARCH 2

SAINT ANGELA OF THE CROSS

(1846–1932) Founder. Born to a humble family in Spain, St. Angela suffered from persistent frail health that forced her to leave the Daughters of Charity. Some years later she received a vision of a vacant cross and knew she was being called to dedicate herself to the poor and sick. Along with three other women, she founded the Sisters of the Company of the Cross and worked tirelessly in service of the poor and sick. Known as Mother of the Poor, she was canonized in May of 2003 by Pope John Paul II.

The nothing keeps silent, the nothing does not want to be, the nothing suffers all. The nothing does not impose itself, the nothing does not command with authority, and finally, the nothing in the creature is practical humility.

—*St. Angela of the Cross*

Love and sensitivity to the poor prompted Saint Angela of the Cross to found her "Company of the Cross" for the most deprived with a charitable and social dimension that made an enormous impact on the Church and society of Seville in her day. Her distinctive traits were naturalness and simplicity, seeking holiness with a spirit of mortification and at the service of God in her brothers and sisters.

—Pope John Paul II, from his homily at the canonization of St. Angela of the Cross

. . . .

MARCH 3

SAINT KATHARINE DREXEL

(1858–1955) Founder. Born into a wealthy Philadelphia family, Katharine was lovingly raised by her father and stepmother who instilled in her a love of God and others. Desiring to help the Native American and African-American communities in need, she founded the Sisters of the Blessed Sacrament and opened many schools, missionary centers, and convents. She spent twenty million dollars of her family fortune to further her charitable work. She died at the age of ninety-six. She was canonized by Pope John Paul II in October of 2000.

If we wish to serve God and love our neighbor well, we must manifest our joy in the service we render to Him and them. Let us open wide our hearts. It is joy which invites us. Press forward and fear nothing.

—St. Katherine Drexel

OPPOSITE: Saint Katharine Drexel

SAINT CASIMIR

(1458–1482) Son of King Casimir IV of Poland, he refused the kingship of Hungary to live a life of prayer, penance, celibacy, and austerity. He died from tuberculosis while in his twenties. He is the patron saint of Poland and Lithuania.

From day to day sing loud thy lay
To Mary's name, O soul of mine;
And freely praise her festal days
And actions of her life divine.

And let thine eyes, in glad surprise,
Gaze on her wondrous dignity;
Sing through the earth the Mother's worth,
And sing the Maiden's purity.

Oh, bend thee low, and pray that thou
Be lightened of thy weight of sin;
Call her to thee, lest the dark sea
Of sin divide and whelm thee in.

Her hand hath given the gifts of Heaven
To us who own her matchless worth;
A Queen Divine, her graces shine
Bright over all in Heaven and earth.

—from hymn to the Blessed Virgin that St. Casimir recited daily,
a handwritten copy of which was buried with him

SAINT JOHN JOSEPH OF THE CROSS

(1654–1734) Religious, priest. Born into wealth and nobility, St. John Joseph left a life of privilege and joined the Franciscans of the Strictest Observance at age sixteen. In the following years he founded a monastery, convent, and was made provincial of the province of Naples. Known for his humility, piety, and religious discipline, St. John Joseph died at the age of eighty.

Abide in peace, banish cares, take no account of all that happens and you will serve God according to his good pleasure and rest in him.

—*St. John Joseph of the Cross*

In the evening of life, we will be judged on love alone.

—*St. John Joseph of the Cross*

SAINT COLETTE

(1380–1447) Religious, founder. Orphaned at seventeen, St. Colette joined the Third Order of St. Francis and lived a solitary, spiritual life. After several years, she had a vision of St. Francis asking her to set about reforming the Poor Clares. Though initially daunted by the task, she persevered and founded seventeen convents under the reformed rule and reformed several others. St. Colette is known for her great holiness, wisdom, and devotion to Jesus in the Eucharist.

We must faithfully keep what we have promised. If through human weakness we fail, we must always without delay arise again by means of holy penance, and give our attention to leading a good life and to dying a holy death. May the Father of all mercy, the Son by his holy passion, and the Holy Spirit, source of peace, sweetness and love, fill us with their consolation. Amen.

—*Prayer of St. Colette*

SAINT PERPETUA
AND SAINT FELICITY

(died c. 203) Martyrs. St. Perpetua was a noblewoman of Carthage, North Africa, and mother of newborn son, and St. Felicity, a slave and expectant mother, was St. Perpetua's maid. Imprisoned for refusing to renounce their faith, they were beheaded at an amphitheater during public games. Perpetua kept a diary that chronicled the anti-Christian persecution during the reign of Septimus Severus. Their martyrdom resonated throughout the early Church, and St. Augustine is said to have preached about it on several occasions.

What a day of horror! Terrible heat, owing to the crowds! Rough treatment by the soldiers! To crown all, I was tormented with anxiety for my baby. . . . Such anxieties I suffered for many days, but I obtained leave for my baby to remain in prison with me, and being relieved of my trouble and anxiety for him, I at once recovered my health, and my prison became a palace to me and I would rather have been there than anywhere else.

—St. Perpetua writing about her imprisonment

SAINT JOHN OF GOD

(1495–1550) Religious. Spending years as a soldier, mercenary, and shepherd, St. John of God was forty years old before he devoted his life to God. He was so intensely repentant for his sins after hearing a sermon from St. John of Avila, that he was placed briefly in an insane asylum. He began caring for the sick and homeless and went on to open a hospital which became the beginnings of the Order of Brothers Hospitalers. He worked tirelessly for ten years in the hospital before he himself succumbed to illness and died on his birthday.

If we look forward to receiving God's mercy, we can never fail to do good so long as we have the strength. For if we share with the poor, out of love for God, whatever he has given to us, we shall receive according to his promise a hundredfold in eternal happiness. What a fine profit, what a blessed reward! With outstretched arms he begs us to turn toward him, to weep for our sins, and to become the servants of love, first for ourselves, then for our neighbors. Just as water extinguishes a fire, so love wipes away sin.

—St. John of God

....

MARCH 9

SAINT DOMINIC SAVIO

(1842–1857) A prayerful and pious child, Dominic went to school run by St. John Bosco when he was twelve. He ardently desired to become a priest and faithfully attended to his studies and in promoting harmony among the other students. He became ill and was sent home from school to recover but his illness only grew worse. He died at the age of fifteen.

Here we make sanctity consist in being joyful all the time and in faithfully performing our duties.

—St. Dominic Savio, letter to a friend

I am seeing wonderful things.

—St. Dominic Savio's last words

SAINT JOHN OGILVIE

(1579–1615) Religious, martyr. Born into a Scottish noble family, St. John Ogilvie was sent to Belgium and Germany for his education. He converted to Catholicism at the age of seventeen and was ordained a priest in Paris in 1610. He returned to Scotland where Catholics were routinely persecuted. He was responsible for many Protestants converting to Catholicism. Betrayed by someone posing as a Catholic, St. John was arrested, imprisoned, and tortured. After several trials, he was convicted of high treason and martyred at the age of thirty-six.

God our Father, fountain of all blessing, we thank you for the countless graces that come to us in answer to the prayers of your saints. With great confidence we ask you in the name of your Son and through the prayers of St. John Ogilvie to help us in all our needs.

Lord Jesus, you chose your servant St. John Ogilvie to be your faithful witness to the spiritual authority of the chief shepherd of your flock. Keep your people always one in mind and heart, in communion with Francis our Pope, and all the bishops of your Church.

Holy Spirit, you gave St. John Ogilvie light to know your truth, wisdom to defend it, and courage to die for it. Through his prayers and example bring our country into the unity and peace of Christ's kingdom. Amen.

—*Novena prayer to St. John Ogilvie*

MARCH 11

SAINT EULOGIUS OF SPAIN

(died c. 859) Priest, martyr. Arrested in 850 during fierce persecutions of Christians by Muslims in Cordova. St. Eulogius was imprisoned along with his bishop and many priests. Although he was freed, he continued to proclaim his faith and harbor other Christians. He was arrested again and condemned to death.

The sacrifice most pleasing to God is contrition of heart.

—*St. Eulogius of Spain*

············

MARCH 12

SAINT SERAPHINA (FINA)

(1238–1253) Virgin. Born to a poor family, she lost her father at a young age and was stricken with a mysterious illness which caused her great pain and left her paralyzed. Her mother passed away suddenly and a neighbor was left to care for the ailing saint. She'd developed a devotion to St. Gregory the Great who had likewise borne much suffering. A vision of St. Gregory came to the girl and she was told her suffering would end on his feast day, March 12. As predicted, St. Seraphina died on March 12, 1253.

Blessed St. Seraphina, you who endured tremendous suffering in your short life, give me the grace to accept my own suffering and to unite my suffering with Jesus as you did so unfailingly. I ask this in the name of Jesus Christ our Lord, Amen.

BLESSED AGNELLUS OF PISA

(died c. 1232) Religious. Blessed Agnellus was received into the Franciscan order by St. Francis himself. St. Francis later sent him to England with a handful of brothers and there they set up convents of their order and added many men to their numbers, some from the most prominent families in England. A paragon of humility and virtue, Blessed Agnellus would often break down and weep during mass and in choir. He died at thirty-eight years of age.

May the Lord bless you.
May the Lord keep you.
May He show His face to you and have mercy.
May He turn to you His countenance and give you peace.
The Lord bless you.

—Blessing of St. Francis

....

SAINT MATILDA

(c. 895–968) Founder. Married to Henry I the Fowler, king of Germany, St. Matilda was a faithful wife, a loving mother, and a generous and humble queen. She established many churches, convents, and monasteries, and was known for her ceaseless almsgiving to the poor. She was venerated as a saint upon her death.

Father in Heaven, St. Matilda was your faithful servant on earth. We thank you for her example to her children but we also thank you for our Queen Mother in heaven, the Blessed Virgin Mary. We pray that through their intercession, all mothers may seek to follow their example. Amen.

SAINT LOUISE DE MARILLAC

(1591–1660) Religious, founder. She was a happily married woman for thirteen years when her husband died, leaving her with a young child. She became a nun and along with St. Vincent de Paul, her spiritual director, founded the Vincentian Sisters of Charity. She is the patron saint of social workers.

If we are assailed by temptations and trials, we become completely dejected, imagining ourselves to be in a deplorable state. And truly, this would be our condition if we did not cling to God by the tip of our souls, saying to Him, from the depths of our hearts, My God, do whatever you will; I belong entirely to you! Despite these temptations, we must perform all our actions purely and simply for the love of God.

—St. Louise de Marillac

SAINT HERLBERT

(c. 970–1021) Priest, archbishop, founder. Highly educated, St. Herlbert was ordained to the priesthood at the age of twenty-four. He was later made the chancellor of Emperor Otto III for Italy and Germany and then archbishop of Cologne. He worked unceasingly to help the poor and the sick of his diocese and devoted much of his time to prayer. He founded a monastery at Deutz where he died and is buried.

Blessed St. Herlbert, you who faithfully served God and performed countless acts of charity for the poor and sick before you, help us to give of ourselves to those in need. We ask that following your example, and that of our Savior, we may always show compassion for the poor and neglected. We ask this in the name of Jesus our Lord, Amen.

SAINT PATRICK

(c. 387–493) Priest, bishop. Kidnapped into slavery from Britain, he spent years in Ireland as a slave. He escaped back to Britain where he was educated and ordained a priest. He returned to Ireland as a bishop and devoted his life to spreading Christianity throughout Ireland. He was responsible for converting thousands of people to Christianity.

Christ to shield me today
Against poison, against burning,
Against drowning, against wounding,
So that there may come to me abundance of reward.
Christ with me, Christ before me, Christ behind me,
Christ in me, Christ beneath me, Christ above me,
Christ on my right, Christ on my left,
Christ when I lie down, Christ when I sit down, Christ when I arise,
Christ in the heart of every man who thinks of me,
Christ in the mouth of everyone who speaks of me,
Christ in every eye that sees me,
Christ in every ear that hears me.

—*from St. Patrick's Breastplate*

SAINT CYRIL OF JERUSALEM

(c. 315–386) Bishop and Doctor of the Church. Bishop of Jerusalem for thirty-five years, St. Cyril spent many years embroiled in combating the Arian heresy which proposed that Jesus was not divine. As a resultof the discord, St. Cyril was exiled from Jerusalem for long periods of time. By his death, the heresy

OPPOSITE: Saint Patrick

had been suppressed due in large part to his unwavering commitment to the true teachings of the Church.

God, eternal shepherd, you tend your Church in many ways and rule us with love. You have chosen your bishops to be shepherds of your flock. Give them a spirit of courage and right judgment, a spirit of knowledge and love. By governing with fidelity those entrusted to their care, may they build your Church as a sign of salvation for the world.

—Prayer for Bishops

. . . .

MARCH 19

SAINT JOSEPH

O blessed St. Joseph, chosen by God to be the foster father and loving guardian of Jesus, chaste spouse of Mary, the Mother of God, and head of the holy family, protect all working people and their families. Intercede for young people who are searching for their place in the world. Be the safe haven for all of us at the hour of death, and guide us safely into heaven. We ask this through Christ our Lord. Amen.

—Prayer to St. Joseph

Saint Joseph was a just man, a tireless worker, the upright guardian of those entrusted to his care. May he always guard, protect and enlighten families.

—Pope John Paul II

Some Saints are privileged to extend to us their patronage with particular efficacy in certain needs, but not in others; but our holy patron St. Joseph has the power to assist us in all cases, in every necessity, in every undertaking.

—St. Thomas Aquinas

MARCH 20

SAINT CUTHBERT

(c. 636–687) Monk, hermit, missionary, bishop. Though he preached to huge crowds as a missionary, St. Cuthbert was content when he received permission to live as a hermit, only to be made a bishop against his will. He spent the last years of his life caring for his flock, caring for the sick, and performing healings for people far and wide.

Great Saint Cuthbert, apostle of the North of England we come to ask for your prayers! Pray for me and for the whole Church of Christ. Pray for all those in need this day and especially for those dear to my heart. Through your great and heroic efforts Christianity has found a home in this land, may it ever be so. You were a man of honor and faith in your own earthly pilgrimage assist me by your powerful intercession to be an honest servant of Christ. I ask you to pray for my special request of if it be God's holy will. O God, you made Your name known to us through the Saints of Northern England. By the intercession of St. Cuthbert, let Your Church continue to grow with an increased number of believers. Grant this through Christ our Lord. Amen.

—*Novena prayer to St. Cuthbert*

·············

MARCH 21

SAINT BENEDICT

(480–543) Abbot. Known as the Father of Western monasticism, he left his home in central Italy to live as a hermit and immerse himself in prayer, austerity, and penance. Another hermit in the area, St. Romanus, mentored him in the ways of Christian asceticism.

His holiness attracted many followers, whom he arranged to live in communal settings under a developing rule. In 529 he founded his great Abbey at Monte Cassino. St. Benedict wrote the tenets of the Rule that formed the foundation for all Western religious orders that came after him. His sister, St. Scholastica, was the first Benedictine nun. St. Benedict died on March 21, 543 after receiving the Eucharist.

What dear brothers, is more delightful than the voice of the Lord calling to us?

—*Rule of St. Benedict, Prologue*

We must know that God regards our purity of heart and tears of compunction, not our many words.

—*Rule of St. Benedict, Chapter 20*

SAINT LEA OF ROME

(died c. 384) Religious. Lea was a Roman noblewoman. When her husband passed away, she renounced her position and joined a convent to live a spare life of prayer and penance. She was a dear friend of St. Jerome, next to whom she was praying when she died.

Who will praise the blessed Lea as she deserves? She renounced painting her face and adorning her head with shining pearls. She exchanged her rich attire for sackcloth, and ceased to command others in order to obey all. She dwelt in a corner with a few bits of furniture; she spent her nights in prayer, and instructed her companions through her example rather than through protests and speeches. And she looked forward to her arrival in heaven in order to receive her recompense for the virtues which she practiced on earth. So it is that thence forth she enjoyed perfect happiness. . . . Hence, I tearfully beg you to refrain from seeking the favors of the world and to renounce all that is carnal. It is impossible to follow both the world and Jesus. Let us live a life of renunciation, for our bodies will soon be dust and nothing else will last any longer.

—*Letter from St. Jerome to St. Marcella announcing St. Lea's death*

....

MARCH 23

SAINT TURIBIUS DE MOGROVEJO

(1538–1606) Archbishop. Born to a noble family in Spain, St. Turibius was well educated and was highly regarded as a professor of law and judge. He was made the missionary archbishop of Peru despite his protestations that he could not serve as a layman. Once ordained, he was sent to Peru, where he championed the rights of the native peoples who were being severely oppressed by the Spanish occupiers. He built schools, churches, hospitals, and founded the first seminary in the Western hemisphere. He is the patron saint of native people's rights and of Latin American bishops.

Time is not our own, and we must give a strict account of it.

—*St. Turibius de Mogrovejo*

....

MARCH 24

SAINT CATHERINE OF SWEDEN

(1330–1381) Religious. Daughter of St. Bridget of Sweden, St. Catherine joined her mother in Rome and, after the death of St. Catherine's husband, the two embarked on many pilgrimages together to many destinations, including Jerusalem. Their lives were focused on prayer, meditation, and on teaching the poor. When her mother died, St. Catherine returned to the convent of the Order of the Holy Savior that her mother had founded and became the superior there until her death.

May the babe of Bethlehem be yours to tend; May the boy of Nazareth be yours to friend; May the man of Galilee his healing send; May the Christ of Calvary his courage lend; May the risen Lord his presence send; And his holy angels defend you, to the end.

—*A Prayer of Pilgrimage to the Holy Land*

....

MARCH 25

THE ANNUNCIATION OF THE LORD

The Angel Gabriel was sent from God to a town of Galilee named Nazareth, to a virgin betrothed to a man named Joseph, of the house of David. The virgin's name was Mary. Upon arriving, the Angel said to her: "Hail, full of grace. The Lord is with you. Blessed are you among women." She was deeply troubled by his words and wondered what his greeting meant. The Angel went on to say to her: "Do not fear, Mary. You have found favor with God. You shall conceive and bear a son and give him the name Jesus. . . . The Holy Spirit will come upon you and the power of the Most High will overshadow you; hence the holy offspring to be born will be called Son of God. . . ." Mary said: "I am the maidservant of the Lord. Let it be done to me as you say."

—*Luke 1:28–38*

....

MARCH 26

SAINT LUCIA FILIPPINI

(1672–1732) Born in Italy and orphaned at a young age, St. Lucia was lovingly raised by relatives and exhibited a wisdom and piety that belied her age. With the patronage of a local cardinal, she formed the Institute of the Religious

Teachers Filippini with the aim of establishing schools for young women from poor families. The schools they founded were intended to promote the dignity of womanhood and healthy family life. In her lifetime, more than fifty schools for girls were established.

Heavenly Father, who promised that all those who instruct others in the ways of holiness will shine as stars for all eternity, fill our hearts and minds with true knowledge and the art of teaching. Give us patience and understanding, justice and prudence, humility and fear of the Lord. Grant us wisdom and charity so that with a pure and holy love of God we ourselves may enjoy all these gifts and impart them to our pupils. Teach our children to be obedient to your laws and docile to your inspirations. Let them be instruments of your peace in their homes, in our land, and in the family of nations as becomes children of the sons of God in the Mystical Body of Christ. May the blessings of your sevenfold Gifts be in all who teach and in all who learn through the Holy Spirit who is the Love of the Father and the Son, our Lord Jesus Christ. Amen.

—*A Prayer for Teachers*

SAINT JOHN OF EGYPT

(304–394) Hermit. A carpenter, St. John was called by God to live in solitude. He preached to crowds from a window in his cell and was responsible for many miraculous cures. He filled his days with intense prayer and spent the last three days of his life without food or water, and was found to have died in prayer.

Believe one who has tried: You shall find a fuller satisfaction in the woods than in books. The trees and the rocks will teach you what you cannot hear from the masters.

—*St. Bernard of Clairvaux*

MARCH 28

SAINT TUTILO

(c. 850–c. 915) Monk, artist, musician. St. Tutilo was an Irish monk who is said to have visited the Abbey of St. Gall on the way home from Rome and decided to stay. He was a painter, musician, sculptor, and architect, though he was exceedingly humble about his work. His paintings and sculptures can still be found in museums and monasteries throughout Europe.

Come, O Creator Spirit, visit our minds, and fill with your grace the hearts you have created. Grant us, we humbly pray, an abundance of that creative inspiration which is the source of every true work of art. May the fruit of our artistic talents transfigure matter and open the human soul to the sense of the eternal and Triune God, who is Father, Son, and Holy Spirit.

Blessed St. Tutilo, you who created beautiful works of art all for the glory of God, pray for us!

....

MARCH 29

SAINT RUPERT OF SALZBURG

(died c. 718). A saint who zealously spread the Good News throughout Austria, Bavaria, and Germany, he founded many churches, convents, and monasteries. He was also instrumental in developing several salt mines. He became the first abbot bishop of Salzburg and is often depicted in art work holding a barrel of salt.

You are the salt of the earth. But if salt loses its taste, with what can it be seasoned? It is no longer good for anything but to be thrown out and trampled underfoot. You are the light of the world.

A city set on a mountain cannot be hidden. Nor they light a lamp and then put it under a bushel basket; it is set on a lamp stand, where it gives light to all in the house. Just so, your light must shine before others, that they may see your good deeds and glorify your heavenly Father.

—*Matthew 5:13–16*

. . . .
MARCH 30

SAINT JOHN CLIMACUS

(525–649) Abbot. Believed to be a disciple of St. Gregory Nazianzen, he joined a monastery on Mount Sinai when he was a teenager and spent forty years living in seclusion—spending his days absorbed in fervent prayer. In his seventies, he was chosen as abbot of the monastery and superior general of all monks and hermits in the country. He later wrote his famous treatise about the rules by which he lived, entitled *The Ladder of Paradise*.

In all your undertakings and in every way of life, whether you are living in obedience, or are not submitting your work to anyone, whether in outward or in spiritual matters, let it be your rule and practice to ask yourself: Am I really doing this in accordance with God's will?

—*St. John Climacus*

. . . .
MARCH 31

BLESSED JOAN OF TOULOUSE

(died c. 1286) Lay Carmelite. She became the first lay associate of the Carmelite order. Though she remained in her own home, she lived faithfully offering prayer and penance in accordance with the Carmelite rule for the rest of her life. When not in prayer, she performed acts of charity and greatly helped those suffering from sickness, poverty, and old age. When Blessed Joan died, she was buried in the Carmelite church of Toulouse, where she'd spent so much of her time deep in prayer.

Vocal prayer must be accompanied by reflection. A prayer in which a person is not aware of Whom he is speaking to; what he is asking; who it is who is asking and of Whom, I don't call prayer—however much the lips may move.

—*St. Teresa of Avila*

APRIL

· · · · · · · · · ·

APRIL 1

SAINT HUGH OF GRENOBLE

(c. 1053–1132) Bishop. A shy and humble man, St. Hugh longed to be a monk but was instead made bishop of Grenoble, a diocese that was in a deplorable state. St. Hugh set about reforming the diocese and having succeeded, he resigned his position and entered a monastery. After only one year, he was recalled by the pope to his flock once more. St. Hugh served as Bishop of Grenoble for fifty-two years. He was canonized by Pope Innocent II only two years after his death.

Some time before his death, he lost his memory for everything but his prayers: the Psalter and the Lord's Prayer he recited with great devotion, almost without intermission: and he was said to have repeated the last three hundred times in one night. Being told that so constant an attention would increase his distemper, he said, "It is quite otherwise: by prayer I always find myself stronger."

—about St. Hugh of Grenoble, from The Lives of the Saints, by Reverend Alban Butler, 1866

We can only learn to know ourselves and do what we can—namely, surrender our will and fulfill God's will in us.

—St. Teresa of Avila

SAINT FRANCIS OF PAOLA

(c. 1416–1508) Hermit, founder. St. Francis was content to live as a hermit in a cave near Paola, Italy. He gathered followers and after seventeen years, he set down a rule and founded the Order of Minims, seeking to get back to the original spirit of St. Francis—embracing poverty, chastity, obedience, and the observance of a perpetual Lenten fast. At the request of the pope, St. Francis traveled to Paris to mentor King Louis XI, who experienced a full conversion as a result of the saint's counsel. While there, St. Francis founded the Order of France. Near the end of his life, he retired to his cell to pray and prepare for his own death, which occurred in his ninety-first year.

Put aside hatred and hostility. See to it that you refrain from harsh words. But if you do speak them, do not be ashamed to apply the remedy from the same lips that inflicted the wounds. In this way you will show each other mercy and not keep alive the memories of past wrongs. Remembering grievances works great damage. It is accompanied by anger, fosters sin, and brings a hatred for justice. It is a rusty arrow spreading poison in the soul. . . . Be lovers of peace, the most precious treasure that anyone can desire. You are already aware that our sins drive God to anger, so you must repent of them, that God in his mercy may spare you. What men conceal is open to God. Turn to him with a sincere heart. Live in such a way that you bring upon yourselves the blessing of God, and that the peace of God our Father may be with you always.

—St. Francis of Paola

APRIL 3

SAINT RICHARD OF CHICHESTER

(1197–1253) Priest, bishop. Orphaned as a child, St. Richard worked his hand at farming before studying at Oxford, Paris, and Bologna. Upon the completion of his studies, he returned to England where he was made chancellor at Oxford. The pope appointed St. Richard the bishop of Chichester against the adamant objections of King Henry III, who vigorously opposed St. Richard until he was threatened with excommunication. Known for his clerical reforms and great charity to the poor, St. Richard was canonized in 1262 by Pope Urban IV.

Thanks be to thee, my Lord Jesus Christ,
for all the benefits thou hast given me,
for all the pains and insults thou hast borne for me.
O most merciful redeemer, friend and brother,
may I know thee more clearly,
love thee more dearly,
and follow thee more nearly, day by day.
Amen.

—Prayer of St. Richard of Chichester

· · · · · · · · ·

APRIL 4

SAINT ISIDORE OF SEVILLE

(c. 560–636) Bishop and Doctor of the Church. With three saints in his immediate family, St. Isidore was perhaps destined for a saintly life. He dedicated his life to the Church at an early age and received an excellent education, sternly supervised by his brother, St. Leander. He went on to succeed St. Leander as bishop of Seville and governed for thirty-seven years. A prolific writer who was conversant in Latin, Greek, and Hebrew, St. Isidore also presided over several important Church Councils in Spain. Sensing his death was imminent, St. Isidore received Holy Communion and distributed all of his money to the poor. He died four days later.

Learning unsupported by grace may get into our ears; it never reaches the heart. But when God's grace touches our innermost minds to bring understanding, His word which has been received by the ear sinks deep into the heart.

—St. Isidore of Seville

. . . .

APRIL 5

SAINT VINCENT FERRER

(c. 1350–1419) Priest. Born to a noble family, St. Vincent entered the Dominican order at nineteen, had a brilliant academic career, and began lecturing in philosophy. The Church was embroiled in the Great Schism during this time, where two men claimed the right to the papacy—one in Rome and one in Avignon. In the midst of this turmoil, St. Vincent was spreading the Good News throughout the world. A fiery speaker, he converted many thousands of people with his legendary preaching. He spent the last twenty years of his life preaching in Spain, France, Italy, Germany, Flanders, England, Scotland, and Ireland. He was canonized in 1455 by Pope Nicholas V.

Whatever you do, think not of yourself, but of God.

—St. Vincent Ferrer

Whoever will proudly dispute and contradict will always stand outside the door. Christ, the master of humility, manifests His truth only to the humble and hides Himself from the proud.

—St. Vincent Ferrer

SAINT JULIANA OF CORNILLON

(1193–1258) Religious, mystic. Orphaned at the age of five, St. Juliana was raised on a farm owned by the convent of Mount Cornillon. She took vows when she was thirteen and later became the prioress of the convent. Possessed with a fervent devotion to the Blessed Sacrament, she received repeated visions about the need for a special feast to honor the Blessed Sacrament. Painfully shy, she waited more than twenty years before acting on these visions. Persecuted by a corrupt official, she was forced into exile and later vindicated, only to be persecuted a second time by the same vicious man. She lived her last years in seclusion. The special feast that she devoted her life to achieving, was adopted by Pope Urban IV who declared the Feast of Corpus Christi a universal feast in 1264.

At sixteen she had her first vision, which was then repeated many times in her Eucharistic adorations. The vision showed the moon in its full splendor, with a dark strip that crossed it diametrically. The Lord made her understand the meaning of what had appeared to her. The moon symbolized the life of the Church on earth; but the opaque line represented the absence of a liturgical feast. Juliana was asked to do her utmost in an effective way to bring about its institution: a feast, namely, in which believers would be able to adore the Eucharist to increase their faith, advance in the practice of virtue and make reparation for offenses to the Most Holy Sacrament.

—Pope Benedict XVI, *remarks about St. Juliana and the origins of the Feast of Corpus Christi, November 2010*

SAINT JOHN BAPTIST DE LA SALLE

(1651–1719) Priest, founder. Born into a noble family and highly educated, St. John was an ordained priest holding a doctorate in theology when he heard God's call to help the poor. Moved by the scores of impoverished children with no opportunity for education, he founded the Brothers of the Christian Schools to train teachers for the poor. In spite of criticism from civil and Church authorities, St. John prevailed and opened up schools throughout France that employed innovative teaching methods and taught both the poor and wealthy delinquent children. In 1950, he was made the patron of all teachers of youth by Pope Pius XII.

How long has Jesus been knocking at the door of your heart, waiting to enter?

—*St. John Baptist de la Salle*

Preach by example, and practice before the eyes of the young what you wish them to accept.

—*St. John Baptist de la Salle*

·········

SAINT JULIE BILLIART

(1751–1816) Religious, founder. As a young woman, St. Julie was paralyzed from a mysterious illness after witnessing an attempt on her father's life. Though bedridden, she spent her days in prayer, contemplation, teaching catechism, and counseling visitors seeking spiritual advice. During the French Revolution, she was forced to go into hiding with the help of friends to escape revolutionaries. Seeing the need for education for the poor and for young girls, she co-founded the Sisters of Notre Dame de Namur. After more than twenty years of paralysis, she was miraculously cured and regained her ability to walk. She spent the rest of her life traveling through France and Belgium opening convents and schools to serve all those in need.

Let us submit in everything to the good pleasure of the good God. We must have crosses, but above all let us not choose them. Let us accept them from the divine hand of the good God. He knows so well the right proportion of our strength. Before all, let us accept them with confidence in his infinite goodness. May that be our only support!

—*St. Julie, letter to one of her sisters, November 8, 1815*

. . . .

APRIL 9

SAINT HEDDA AND HIS COMPANIONS

(died c. 870) Abbot, martyr. St. Hedda was the Benedictine abbot of the monastery at Peterborough in England. In 865, the Vikings, who had a particular hatred of Christians, raided the monastery at Peterborough, killed St. Hedda and the eighty-four monks residing there, and burned the monastery to the ground.

Our friends, then, are all those who unjustly afflict upon us trials and ordeals, shame and injustice, sorrows and torments, martyrdom and death; we must love them greatly for we will possess eternal life because of what they bring upon us.

—*St. Francis of Assisi*

God does not require of us the martyrdom of the body; he requires only the martyrdom of the heart and the will.

—*St. John Vianney*

APRIL 10

BLESSED ANTHONY NEYROT

(c. 1425–1460). Religious, martyr. Born in northern Italy, Blessed Anthony was received into the Dominican Order by St. Antoninus. While he was sailing from Sicily to Naples, his ship was overtaken by Moorish pirates who brought him to Tunis in North Africa where he was imprisoned for his faith. To gain his freedom, he renounced Christianity, converted, and even married. Severely repentant several months later, he sent his wife back to her family, donned his Dominican habit and began publicly preaching and expressing sorrow for his sins. The emir ordered him killed on the spot and he was stoned to death.

There is still time for endurance, time for patience, time for healing, time for change. Have you slipped? Rise up. Have you sinned? Cease. Do not stand among sinners, but leap aside. For when you turn away and weep, then you will be saved.

—St. Basil the Great

Even if you are committing mortal sins, keep on praying, and I guarantee you that you will reach the harbor of salvation.

—St. Teresa of Avila

....

APRIL 11

SAINT GEMMA GALGANI

(1878–1903) Mystic. Born to a humble family in Tuscany, St. Gemma developed a love of prayer at a young age. Though her frail health prevented her from joining a religious community, she was gifted with many mystical experiences during prayer, and bore the stigmata until three years before her death. Having contracted tuberculosis, she suffered greatly and died at the age of twenty-five on Holy Saturday. She was canonized in 1940.

OPPOSITE: Saint Gemma Galgani

O Jesus, if I but considered attentively your immense solicitude for me, how greatly should I not excel in every virtue? Pardon me, O Jesus, so much carelessness, pardon such great ignorance. My God, Jesus my Love, Increated Goodness, what would have become of me if you had not drawn me to yourself? Open your heart to me, open to me your sacramental breast; I open mine to you.

—St. Gemma Galgani

. . . .

APRIL 12

SAINT JOSEPH MOSCATI

(1880–1927) Medical doctor. Drawn to medicine after witnessing his brother suffer the effects of a traumatic brain injury, St. Joseph Moscati studied medicine and became a well-known medical doctor, hospital administrator, professor, and biochemistry pioneer. He was also a faith-filled man who attended daily mass, lived a chaste life, and performed countless acts of charity for his patients. During World War I, he visited and treated 3,000 wounded veterans, and routinely treated the poor at no charge. Known as the Holy Physician of Naples, St. Joseph Moscati continued working tirelessly for his patients until his death at the age of forty-six. He was canonized by Pope John Paul II in October 1987, the first modern medical doctor to be canonized.

Remember that you have to deal not only with the bodies but also with the moaning souls coming to you. How many suffering people you will more easily soothe by advising and going straight to their souls, instead of giving good prescriptions to be given to the chemist! Be joyful because great will be your reward; but you will have to set a good example of your elevation to God.

—St. Joseph Moscati

SAINT MARTIN I

(died c. 656) Pope, martyr. The last pope to be venerated as a martyr, St. Martin I spent much of his papacy battling the Monothelite heresy which denied the humanity of Christ. St. Martin's refusal to accept this heresy inflamed the emperor who had him kidnapped, imprisoned, and exiled in Crimea. After two years in exile, St. Martin died.

What fear hath seized all these men, which can hinder them from fulfilling the commands of God, in relieving the distressed? Have I appeared such an enemy to the whole church, or to them in particular? However, I pray God, by the intercession of St. Peter, to preserve them steadfast and immovable in the orthodox faith. As to this wretched body, God will have care of it. He is at hand; why should I give myself any trouble? I hope in his mercy, he will not prolong my course.

—*St. Martin I, letter to a friend from prison*

SAINT KATERI TEKAKWITHA

(c. 1656–1680) Virgin. The daughter of a Mohawk warrior, she was orphaned at a young age when the small pox epidemic took her parents, and left her disfigured and partially blind. Adopted by an aunt and uncle, she converted to Christianity as a teenager and incurred the wrath of her tribe as a result. Fearing for her life, she embarked on a 200-mile journey on-foot to a Christian colony of Native Americans in Canada. There, she spent her life in prayer, undergoing acts of severe penance, and engaging in charitable acts for the old and sick. Dying at the age of twenty-four, she is known as the Lily of the Mohawks and was canonized in October 2012 by Pope Benedict XVI.

I am not my own; I have given myself to Jesus. He must be my only love. The state of helpless poverty that may befall me if I do not marry does not frighten me. All I need is a little food and a few pieces of clothing. With the work of my hands I shall always earn what is necessary and what is left over I'll give to my relatives and to the poor. If I should become sick and unable to work, then I shall be like the Lord on the cross. He will have mercy on me and help me, I am sure.

—St. Kateri Tekakwitha

· · · · · · · · · ·

APRIL 15

SAINT DAMIEN OF MOLOKAI

(1840–1889) Priest. A missionary priest, St. Damien spent sixteen years ministering to the exiled leprosy patients in Molokai, Hawaii. He attended to their physical and spiritual needs with kindness and compassion, and worked unceasingly to secure the medical services and funding they desperately needed. He eventually contracted the deadly disease himself and died on April 15, 1889; thus known as a "martyr of charity." St. Damien was canonized by Pope Benedict XVI in 2009.

The sacrifice is great for a heart which tenderly loves his parents, family, religious brothers, and the land where he was born. But the voice which invites us, which has called us to make the offering of everything we have, is the voice of God Himself. It is our Divine Savior Who says to us as to His first apostles: "Go, teach all nations, instructing them to observe all my commandments. . . "

—St. Damien of Molokai

Having no doubts about the true nature of the disease, I am calm, resigned, and very happy in the midst of my people. God certainly knows what is best for my sanctification and I gladly repeat: "Thy will be done."

—St. Damien of Molokai

SAINT BENEDICT JOSEPH LABRE

(1748–1783) Wandering holy man. After several failed attempts at monastic life, St. Benedict Joseph heard God's call to dedicate his life to spiritual pilgrimage. He spent four years traveling through Europe, visiting the great shrines, praying fervently, and living in extreme poverty. He ended his holy journey in Rome, where he would sleep in the Colosseum at night and spend hours in prayer in churches during the day. This saintly wanderer died peacefully in Rome at the age of thirty-five. He was canonized in 1883 by Pope Leo XIII.

One of the first signs of a saint may well be the fact that other people do not know what to make of him. In fact, they are not sure whether or not he is crazy or only proud; but it must at least be pride to be haunted by some individual ideal which nobody but God really comprehends. . . . He cannot seem to make his life fit in with the books. Sometimes his case is so bad that no monastery will keep him. He has to be dismissed, sent back to the world, like Benedict Joseph Labre, who wanted to be a Trappist and a Carthusian and succeeded in neither. He finally ended up as a tramp. He died in some street in Rome. And yet the only canonized saint, venerated by the whole Church, who lived either as a Cisterican or a Carthusian since the Middle Ages is St. Benedict Joseph Labre.

—Thomas Merton, *New Seeds of Contemplation*

SAINT STEPHEN HARDING

(c. 1060–1134) Abbot. A scholar, St. Stephen heard God's call and joined the monastery of Molesme in Burgandy of which St. Robert was the abbot. Desiring to live under a stricter rule, a number of them left and established a new monastery at Citeaux. They lived an austere life of work, strict poverty, and observed a rule of silence. In 1112, St. Bernard of Clairveaux came to the order bringing others with him. Known as the Father of the Cistercian Order, St. Stephen drafted the Charter of Clarity which set forth the rule for the order and he served as abbot for twenty-five years. St. Stephen was canonized in 1623.

O Blessed St. Stephen Harding, whose life of work, prayer, and poverty sought to emulate that of our Savior, help us to do God's work with the discipline and focus that guided you. We ask this in the name of Jesus Christ. Amen.

· · · · · · · · · ·

BLESSED MARIE-ANNE BLONDIN

(1809–1890) Religious, founder. Born to a devout French-Canadian farm family, Blessed Marie-Anne was a pious child who learned how to read and write while she worked as a domestic servant for a nearby religious order. Desiring to teach the illiterate farm children, she proposed the radical concept of teaching boys and girls in the same school. She acquired the necessary permission and at the age of thirty-nine she founded the Sisters of St. Anne for this purpose. Despite being the founder and superior of the Order, she was stymied by the chaplain of the congregation, who had her removed for reasons unknown. After this demotion, she spent the last thirty-two years of her life obediently working in the laundry and ironing room for her Order.

The deeper a tree sinks its roots into the soil, the greater its chances of growing, branching out, and bearing fruit.

—*Blessed Marie-Anne Blondin, in answer to a novice who asked her why she, the founder of the Order, was doing the laundry*

SAINT GEROLD

(died 978) Hermit. Born to a noble family, St. Gerold turned his back on the world and dedicated his life to God. He gave his land to the monastery where he sons were monks and lived the rest of his life as a hermit in the forest.

Thus walking on this way with an awakened heart, not only do we escape the heavy cares of this world, but we are uplifted above ourselves and do taste of the divine sweetness.

—*St. Angela of Foligno*

SAINT AGNES OF MONTEPULCIANO

(c. 1268–1317) Born to a wealthy family, St. Agnes was a holy child who begged her parents to let her enter the convent. At the age of nine she entered the monastery near her home. At thirteen, she was sent with some other sisters to establish a new convent in Procena, where she was elected abbess of the community when she was only twenty. In 1306 she was recalled home to head the community at Montepulciano. Known for her deep contemplative prayer life, she once had a vision, where the Blessed Mother appeared to her with the infant Jesus and let St. Agnes hold and caress the baby. She died on April 20th at the age of forty-nine. Years later, when her body was moved it was found to be incorrupt. One of the many pilgrims to her tomb was St. Catherine of Siena.

O God, who adorned Agnes, Your bride, with a marvelous fervor in prayer, grant that by imitating her example, we may always hold fast to You in spirit, and so come to enjoy the abundant fruits of holiness. Through Our Lord Jesus Christ Your Son, Who lives and reigns with You in the unity of the Holy Spirit, one God for ever and ever. Amen.

—*Prayer honoring St. Agnes of Montepulciano*

SAINT ANSELM OF CANTERBURY

(c. 1033–1109) Bishop and Doctor of the Church. He joined the monastery at Bec when he was twenty-seven and was made prior and then abbot in 1078. A brilliant philosopher and theologian, he was made Archbishop of Canterbury in 1093. An ardent defender of the faith, he wrote some of the most important and influential works in all of Catholic philosophy.

Why, then has the fool said in his heart, there is no God, when it is so evident, to a rational mind, that thou dost exist in the highest degree of all? Why, except that he is dull and a fool?

—*St. Anselm of Canterbury*

Faith seeks understanding. I do not seek to understand that I may believe, but I believe in order to understand.

—*St. Anselm of Canterbury*

SAINT MAREAS AND HIS COMPANIONS

(died c. 342) Martyrs. St. Mareas was the Bishop of Persia who was martyred together with twenty-one other bishops and two-hundred-fifty monks, nuns, and lay people under King Shapur II. This violent extirpation of early Christians nearly brought Christianity in Persia to an end.

The martyrs were bound, imprisoned, scourged, racked, burned, torn apart, butchered—and they multiplied.

—*St. Augustine of Hippo*

I am God's wheat, and I am being ground by the teeth of wild beasts to make a pure loaf for Christ.

—*St. Ignatius of Antioch*

....

APRIL 23

SAINT GEORGE

(died c. 303) Martyr. It is believed that St. George was a soldier in the army of Diocletian. Upon his conversion to Christianity, he bravely confronted the emperor and was tortured and martyred as a result. St. George was made the patron of England in 1222. He is usually depicted in battle with a dragon.

St. George, heroic Catholic soldier and defender of your Faith, you dared to criticize a tyrannical Emperor and were subjected to horrible torture. You could have occupied a high military position but you preferred to die for your Lord. Obtain for us the great grace of heroic Christian courage that should mark soldiers of Christ. Amen.

—*Prayer to St. George*

....

APRIL 24

SAINT FIDELIS OF SIGMARINGEN

(1577–1622) St. Fidelis was a successful lawyer when he dedicated his life to God, gave away his possessions, and joined the Capuchin Order. He journeyed to Switzerland where he preached the Good News and converted many to Catholicism. Confronted with an angry mob who threatened his life if he did not renounce his faith, St. Fidelis was attacked and killed, praying for his persecutors until the end. He was canonized in 1746.

From now on I want to live in complete poverty, chastity, and obedience amidst sufferings and persecutions and in austere penance and profound humility. I came from the womb of my mother with nothing, and with nothing I desire to return to the arms of my Savior.

—*St. Fidelis of Sigmaringen*

SAINT MARK THE EVANGELIST

The writer of the second Gospel, St. Mark was highly regarded in the early Christian church. Although not one of the original twelve apostles, St. Mark did live during the time of Jesus, and was related to the apostle, St. Barnabas. He traveled through Cyprus with St. Paul and St. Barnabas to spread the Good News and converted thousands of people to Christianity. He was a close disciple of St. Peter who referred to him as "my son." It is believed Mark's gospel was based upon the accounts of St. Peter. Mark was made the first bishop of Alexandria and martyred there. He is the patron saint of Venice.

Almighty God, who by the hand of Mark the Evangelist have given to your Church the Gospel of Jesus Christ the Son of God: We thank you for this witness, and pray that we may be firmly grounded in its truth; through Jesus Christ our Lord, who lives and reigns with You and the Holy Spirit, one God, for ever and ever.

—*Prayer honoring St. Mark the Evangelist*

APRIL 26

SAINT CLETUS

(died c. 91) Pope. Believed to be the third successor to St. Peter, he is said to have led the Church for twelve years and ordained many priests to lead the fledgling Church. He likely died a martyr during the Roman Empire's persecution of Christians and is buried next to his predecessor, St. Linus, who is buried next to St. Peter.

O Blessed St. Pope Cletus, you led the Church from the earliest days of our faith and who died a martyr's death, pray for us! Amen.

OPPOSITE: Saint Mark the Evangelist

SAINT ZITA

(1218–1278) Mystic. Born to a humble but pious home, St. Zita was sent by her family into domestic service at the age of twelve. She worked for a wealthy family for decades. A hard worker, she always made time for prayer and for works of charity to those in need. Known for her mystical prayer experiences, she was venerated as a saint locally upon her death and canonized in 1696 by Pope Innocent II. She is the patron of domestic workers.

O glorious Joseph! Who concealed your incomparable and regal dignity of custodian of Jesus and of the Virgin Mary under the humble appearance of a craftsman and provided for them with your work, protect with loving power your sons, especially entrusted to you.

You know their anxieties and sufferings, because you yourself experienced them at the side of Jesus and of His Mother. Do not allow them, oppressed by so many worries, to forget the purpose for which they were created by God. Do not allow the seeds of distrust to take hold of their immortal souls. Remind all the workers that in the fields, in factories, in mines, and in scientific laboratories, they are not working, rejoicing, or suffering alone, but at their side is Jesus, with Mary, His Mother and ours, to sustain them, to dry the sweat of their brow, giving value to their toil. Teach them to turn work into a very high instrument of sanctification as you did. Amen.

—*Prayer written by Pope John XXIII*
entrusting workers to St. Joseph

SAINT PETER CHANEL

(1802–1841) Priest, martyr. The son of humble French farmers, St. Peter Chanel became a Marist priest and the first missionary to the South Pacific. After three years of trying to convert the people of Fortuna in the New Hebrides, he baptized the son of the chief. Infuriated, the chief sent a band of warriors to kill him. He died with the words, "It is well for me that you do this thing." St. Peter's life and death made a deep impression on the native population who converted to Christianity and remains Christian to this day. St. Peter Chanel was canonized in 1954 by Pope Pius XII.

O glorious St. Peter Chanel, your reliance on our most Blessed Mother makes you a perfect model of Marian simplicity. Inspire me to work humbly for others and to care for them with love that, through me, they may experience our Holy Father's love and care. Amen.

—*Prayer to St. Peter Chanel*

SAINT CATHERINE OF SIENA

(1347–1380) Religious, mystic, Doctor of the Church. The twenty-third child in her family, St. Catherine started receiving spiritual visions at the age of six. Growing more devout with age, she rejected her mother's entreaties to make a suitable marriage and joined the Dominican Third Order when she was seventeen. Her growing reputation for holiness and charity led many followers to her. A brilliant spiritual writer, she famously counseled Pope Gregory XI to return the papacy from Avignon to Rome. She spent the last years of her life working to unify the Church from the Great Schism, and died at the age of thirty-three. Her body was found to be incorrupt in 1430. In 1970, she was made a Doctor of the Church along with St. Teresa of Avila.

In your nature, eternal Godhead, I shall come to know my nature. And what is my nature, boundless Love? It is fire, because you are nothing but a fire of love. And you have given humankind a share in this nature for by the fire of love you created us.

—St. Catherine of Siena

God said: They are My anointed ones, and I call them My Christs, because I have given them the office of administering Me to you, and have placed them like fragrant flowers in the mystical body of the holy Church. The angel himself has no such dignity, for I have given it to those men whom I have chosen for my ministers, and whom I have appointed as earthly angels in this life.

—St. Catherine of Siena

Take care that I do not have to complain about you to Jesus crucified. There is no one else I can complain to, for you have no superior on earth.

—Letter from St. Catherine of Siena to Pope Gregory XI

· · · · · · · · · ·

APRIL 30

SAINT PIUS V

(1504–1572) Religious, priest, bishop, cardinal, pope. Born to a poor family, St. Pius joined the Dominican Order as a teenager, and was ordained a priest in 1528. Of a deeply humble nature, he somehow rose through the liturgical ranks and was elected pope in 1566. Once elected pope, he embarked on widespread Church reform. Much of his six-year papacy was devoted to battling heresy— be it the advancing Turkish armies or Protestantism. He is responsible for establishing the Feast of the Holy Rosary after the impossible victory against the Turks at the Battle of Lepanto through the intercession of The Blessed Mother.

OPPOSITE: Saint Catherine of Siena

Some people are so foolish that they think they can go through life without the help of the Blessed Mother. Love the Madonna and pray the rosary, for her Rosary is the weapon against the evils of the world today. All graces given by God pass through the Blessed Mother.

—St. Padre Pio

My impression is that the Rosary is of the greatest value not only according to the words of Our Lady of Fatima, but according to the effects of the Rosary one sees throughout history. My impression is that Our Lady wanted to give ordinary people, who might not know how to pray, this simple method of getting closer to God.

—Sister Lucia dos Santos, one of the children of Fatima

BLESSED PAULINE VON MALLINCKRODT

(1817–1881) Religious, founder. Born into a privileged German family, Blessed Pauline had a special concern for the poor from an early age. She was known to pick up pieces of broken glass on her way to school so barefoot children would not step on it. Caring for her three younger siblings after her mother died, she opened a nursery for children in 1840. She later took on several blind students and began her lifelong ministry to the blind. A devoted educator, she founded the Sisters of Christian Charity in 1849 whose sisters continue today to focus on education, health care, and social work. Mother Pauline died on April 30, 1881 at the age of sixty-four. She was declared Blessed by Pope John Paul II on April 14, 1985.

It does not matter whether a thing is difficult or easy, convenient or inconvenient. If it is God's will, it must be done. That settles it!

—Blessed Pauline von Mallinckrodt

MAY

....

SAINT JOSEPH THE WORKER

Those who give themselves to prayer should in a special manner have always a devotion to St. Joseph; for I know not how any man can think of the Queen of the angels, during the time that she suffered so much with the Infant Jesus, without giving thanks to St. Joseph for the services he rendered them then.

—St. Teresa of Avila

We should, indeed, honor St. Joseph, since the Son of God Himself was graciously pleased to honor him by calling him father. The Holy Scriptures speak of him as the father of Jesus. "His father and mother were marveling at the things spoken—concerning Him" (Luke 2:33). Mary also used this name: "in sorrow thy father and I have been seeking thee" (Luke 2:48). If, then, the King of Kings was pleased to raise Joseph to so high a dignity, it is right and obligatory on our part to endeavor to honor him as much as we can.

—St. Alphonsus Liguori

....

MAY 2

SAINT ATHANASIUS

(c. 296–373) Bishop and Doctor of the Church. Born in Alexandria and later made the Bishop of his birthplace, St. Athanasius fought mightily against the Arian heresy, which denied the divinity of Christ. He endured many trials and persecutions as a result, including attempts on his life and many years in exile. Considered one of the most important men of his times, St. Athanasius died peacefully on May 2, 373.

The Lord did not come to make a display. He came to heal and to teach suffering men. For one who wanted to make a display the thing would have been just to appear and dazzle the beholders. But for Him Who came to heal and to teach the way was not merely to dwell here, but to put Himself at the disposal of those who needed Him, and to be manifested according as they could bear it, not vitiating the value of the Divine appearing by exceeding their capacity to receive it.

—St. Athanasius, on the Incarnation

. . . .

MAY 3

SAINT PHILIP

(died c. 80) Apostle. St. Philip was one of the first apostles called by Jesus. As with the other apostles, the Gospels reveal that Philip needed time to make sense of who Jesus was and what his mission would be. After the Ascension, St. Philip is said to have preached the Gospel in Greece, Phrygia, and Syria. He was most likely martyred.

SAINT JAMES

(died c. 62) Apostle. St. James, son of Alphaeus is one of the original twelve apostles, but not much is known about him except that Jesus chose him to be a "pillar" of the Church. He is known as James the Less, James Minor, or James the Younger to distinguish him from James the son of Zebedee.

O God, grant us through the prayers of the Apostles Philip and James, a share in the Passion and Resurrection of your Only Begotten Son, so that we may merit to behold you for eternity. Through our Lord Jesus Christ, your Son, who lives and reigns with you in the unity of the Holy Spirit, one God, for ever and ever.

—Prayer honoring St. Philip and St. James

BLESSED MARIE-LEONIE PARADIS

(1840–1912) The child of a poor but devout family in Quebec, Blessed Marie-Leonie was educated by the Sisters of Notre Dame and joined the Sisters of the Congregation of the Holy Cross in 1854. For years she taught, both in Canada and in the United States, but she finally realized her dream of establishing an order for the support of the priesthood. In 1880, she founded The Little Sisters of the Holy Family, an order dedicated to the domestic needs and support of priests and seminarians. She led the order for more than thirty years and left six-hundred sisters when she died at the age of seventy-two. Blessed Marie-Leonie was beatified in 1984 by Pope John Paul II.

My confidence in our good Mother is unlimited. She knows our needs and has such great power over the heart of her divine Son.

—*Blessed Marie-Leonie Paradis*

Let us work, my daughters, we shall rest in heaven!

—*Blessed Marie-Leonie Paradis*

SAINT JUDITH OR JUTTA OF PRUSSIA

(c. 1200–1260) Hermit. Born into the German aristocracy, St. Judith married a wealthy nobleman when she was fifteen. She lived and dressed simply despite their wealth and gave generously to the poor. Her husband died unexpectedly while they were on a religious pilgrimage, and she lovingly raised their children on her own, each of whom entered a monastery when old enough. Discerning a new vocation, St. Judith gave away her possessions, and moved to Prussia to live the remainder of her life as a hermit. She spent her days in prayer and in aiding the sick and travelers. St. Judith is the patron of Prussia and of widows.

Three things can lead us close to God. They are painful physical suffering, being in exile in a foreign land, and being poor by choice because of love for God.

—St. Judith of Prussia

. . . .

MAY 6

BLESSED FRANÇOIS DE MONTMORENCY LAVAL

(1623–1708) Priest, bishop. Born in a small town in France, Blessed François was educated by the Jesuits and ordained in 1647. He was made the first bishop of Quebec City in 1658, and given the enormous job of organizing the Catholic Church in Canada. A faithful and caring leader, Blessed Francois set up parishes for the French inhabitants and established the seminary of Quebec in 1663. After his retirement, he dedicated the last twenty years of his life to works of charity and spiritual guidance. He died reciting the rosary and the Litany of the Holy Family. Bishop Laval was declared blessed in 1980 by Pope John Paul II.

Lord Jesus Christ, watch over your missionaries—priests, religious, and lay people—who leave everything to give testimony to your word and your love. In difficult moments, sustain their energies, comfort their hearts, and crown their work with spiritual achievements. Let the adorable image of you crucified on the Cross, which accompanies them throughout life, speak to them of heroism, generosity, love and peace. Amen.

—Prayer for Missionaries

. . . .

MAY 7

BLESSED GISELE

(985–1065) Religious. Married to St. Stephen of Hungary, Blessed Gisele gave birth to a son who would become St. Emeric. After the death of her husband,

Blessed Gisele retreated to the Benedictine Abbey of Niedurburg of which she became the abbess. The rest of her life was spent in prayer and penance. She was declared blessed in 1975.

She who is truly a widow, left all alone, has set her hope on God and continues in supplications and prayers night and day.

—*1 Timothy, 5:5*

·······
MAY 8

BLESSED JULIAN OF NORWICH

(c. 1342–1413) Mystic. A beloved English mystic, Blessed Julian received a series of sixteen revelations on such subjects as the love of God, the Incarnation, the Redemption, and Divine Consolation that she set down in manuscript form in *Sixteen Revelations of Divine Love.* She lived a prayerful, reclusive life outside of the walls of St. Julian's Church, and her reputation for sanctity drew many pilgrims to her. Though she was never formally beatified, she is venerated as Blessed.

There is no creature made who can realize how much, how sweetly, and how tenderly our Maker loves us. And therefore we can, with His grace and His help, stand in spirit, gazing with endless wonder at this lofty, immeasurable love—beyond human scope—that the Almighty, in His goodness, has for us.

—*Blessed Julian of Norwich*

·······
MAY 9

BLESSED NICHOLAS ALBERGATI

(died 1443) Monk, bishop, archbishop, cardinal. Blessed Nicholas joined the Carthusian Order at the age of twenty. He was somewhat reluctantly elevated to bishop, archbishop, and cardinal. He preferred living simply and was diligent in attending to the pastoral needs of his flock—taking the time to visit their homes and tend to their practical and spiritual needs. As he rose within the liturgical ranks, he became a great diplomat and negotiated agreements on behalf of several popes with various heads of state. Known as a wise spiritual leader, Blessed Nicholas was beatified in 1744.

Heavenly Father,
Help me to hear your call. Help me to understand what your plan
is for me.
And give me the courage to answer your call. I ask this in your
name, Amen.

—*A Prayer for Vocations*

. . . .
MAY 10

SAINT JOHN OF AVILA

(c. 1499–1569) Priest and Doctor of the Church. A brilliant student of philosophy and theology, St. John of Avila was ordained a priest and spread the word of God for nine years as a missionary in Spain. A gifted preacher, spiritual advisor, confessor, and mystical writer, he gave spiritual guidance to St. Teresa of Avila, St. John of the Cross, St. Francis Borgia, and St. Peter of Alcantara. Canonized in 1970, St. John of Avila was declared a Doctor of the Church in 2012.

Christ tells us that if we want to join Him, we shall travel the way He took. It is surely not right that the Son of God should go His way on the path of shame while the sons of men walk the way of worldly honor.

—*St. John of Avila*

Turn yourself round like a piece of clay and say to the Lord: I am clay, and you, Lord, the potter. Make of me what you will.

—*St. John of Avila*

SAINT IGNATIUS OF LACONI

(1701–1781) Monk. Born to a poor by devout family, St. Ignatius joined the Franciscan Order after he was spared from a near-death experience and was convinced that God was calling him to a religious life. He was an obedient and humble brother. He worked for fifteen years in the weaving shed and then for forty years going door to door asking for donations to help sustain the order. But what he gave was as vital as what he received; his visits to the sick and lonely proved to be a great blessing. He died at the age of eighty, beloved and already venerated as a saint. He was canonized in 1951.

Most high, Glorious God,
enlighten the darkness of my heart
and give me, Lord, a correct faith, a certain hope,
a perfect charity, sense and knowledge,
so that I may carry out Your holy and true command.

—First recorded prayer of St. Francis, when as a
young man he struggled to discern his vocation

SAINT NEREUS, SAINT ACHILLEUS, AND SAINT PANCRAS

(first century) Martyrs. St. Nereus and St. Achilleus were believed to be Roman soldiers who converted to Christianity and were martyred for their faith. Other sources indicate that they were servants to Flavia Domitilla, the niece of Emperors Titus and Domitian. It is believed that when she converted to Christianity, she was martyred together with St. Nereus and St. Achilleus. St. Pancras, of noble birth, was baptized when he was fourteen and began to give all of his possessions to the poor. When he refused to abandon his faith, St. Pancras was martyred in the year 304.

I pray, my brother, that we may be found worthy to be cursed, censured, and ground down, and even to be executed in the name of Jesus Christ, as long as Christ Himself is not killed in us.

—St. Paulinus of Nola

....

MAY 13

OUR LADY OF FATIMA

My impression is that the Rosary is of the greatest value not only according to the words of Our Lady of Fatima, but according to the effects of the Rosary one sees throughout history. My impression is that Our Lady wanted to give ordinary people, who might not know how to pray, this simple method of getting closer to God.

—Sister Lucia, to whom Our Lady of Fatima appeared

Mary is our great helper; she it is, who presents to her divine Son, all our prayers, our tears, and our sighs; she it is, who obtains the graces for us which we need for our sanctification.

—St. John Vianney

If you ever feel distressed during your day—call upon our Lady— just say this simple prayer: "Mary, Mother of Jesus, please be a mother to me now." I must admit—this prayer has never failed me.

—Blessed Mother Teresa of Calcutta

....

MAY 14

SAINT MATTHIAS

(died c. 80) Apostle. St. Matthias was the apostle chosen by the eleven to replace Judas Iscariot after Judas's betrayal of Jesus and his suicide. It is believed that the eleven gathered together after Jesus' Ascension but before the descent of the

Holy Spirit at Pentecost and chose Matthias from between him and one other candidate to complete their number. As the apostles required, Matthias had been baptized by John the Baptist, was a follower of Jesus throughout his entire ministry, and a witness to his resurrection.

O Glorious St. Matthias, in God's design it fell upon you to take the place of the unfortunate Judas who betrayed his Master. You were selected by the twofold sign of the uprightness of your life and the call of the Holy Spirit. Obtain for us the grace to practice the same uprightness of life and to be called by that same Spirit to wholehearted service of the Church. Then, after a life of zeal and good works, let us be ushered into your company in heaven to sing forever the praises of Father, Son, and Holy Spirit.

—Prayer to St. Matthias

MAY 15

SAINT ISIDORE THE FARMER

(c. 1070–1130) Farm laborer. Born to a peasant family near Madrid, Spain St. Isidore worked in the fields for a wealthy landowner his entire life. He attended daily Mass and found time to help the poor and animals despite his long hours of farm work. He was blessed with spiritual visions, and it is said that angels sometimes helped him complete his work in the fields. The patron of Madrid, farmers, peasants, and laborers, St. Isidore, a simple man with a profound faith, was canonized in 1622.

Blessed St. Isidore, you know how normal it is to cultivate the land for you were employed as a farm laborer most of your life. Although you received God's help materially through Angels in the field, all farmers are aided spiritually to see the wonders God has strewn on this earth. Encourage all farmers in their labors and help them to feed many people. Amen.

—Prayer to St. Isidore

SAINT BRENDAN THE VOYAGER

(died c. 577) Priest, monk. This Irish saint founded many monasteries and churches in Ireland. While St. Brendan surely traveled to places such as Scotland, Wales, and England, spreading the Good News, legend has it that he voyaged with his monks for seven years in search of the Promised Land and possibly traveled as far as North America. One of the Twelve Apostles of Ireland, St. Brendan is the patron saint of boatmen, mariners, sailors, travelers, and watermen.

Help me to journey beyond the familiar
and into the unknown.
Give me the faith to leave old ways
and break fresh ground with You.

Christ of the mysteries, I trust You
to be stronger than each storm within me.
I will trust in the darkness and know
that my times, even now, are in Your hand.
Tune my spirit to the music of heaven,
and somehow, make my obedience count for You.

—The Prayer of St. Brendan

SAINT PASCHAL BAYLON

(1540–1592) Franciscan lay brother. St. Paschal was a mystic even as a child, and joined the Franciscan Order after receiving a vision. Devout and humble, St. Paschal had a fervent devotion to the Eucharist and was named the patron of all Eucharistic confraternities and Congresses in 1897. He was canonized in 1690. Since 1969 his veneration has been limited to local calendars.

Every day He humbles Himself just as He did when He came from His heavenly throne into the Virgin's womb; every day He comes to us and lets us see Him in lowliness, when He descends from the bosom of the Father into the hands of the priest at the altar.

—St. Francis of Assisi

SAINT JOHN I

(died 526) Pope, martyr. Saint John I was elected pope in 523. The ruler of Italy at that time, King Theodoric, an adherent to the Arian heresy of Christianity, compelled the saint to travel to meet with the emperor of Constantinople, Justin I, to ensure fair treatment of the Arians. Though the mission was successful, Theodoric feared that Saint John had conspired with Justin I against him. He thus had the saint kidnapped and imprisoned where he died from starvation.

I am not afraid. I have been waiting for my Lord for a long time. He is the one who has made me love death and now my one desire is to go and be with Him.

—Blessed Rafka al-Rayes

I feel in me the vocation of the Priest. I have the vocation of the Apostle. Martyrdom was the dream of my youth, and this dream has grown with me. Considering the mystical body of the Church, I desired to see myself in them all.

—St. Thérèse of Lisieux

SAINT CELESTINE V

(c. 1210–1296) Hermit, pope. One of twelve children, St. Celestine was a pious child who once told his mother he would end up as a saint. At the age of twenty, he became a hermit and lived a life of fervent prayer and penance. At the age of eighty-four, he was elected pope. After four or five months, St. Celestine stepped down, believing he was not leading the Church effectively. Though he desired to return to his hermitage, he was held in a castle where he died within a short time from neglect. St. Celestine V was canonized in 1313.

Heavenly Father, you called blessed Celestine to serve you humbly both as pope and hermit. By his intercession may we follow the hard road that leads to eternal life. We ask this through Jesus Christ Our Lord and Savior. Amen.

—*Prayer honoring St. Celestine V*

SAINT BERNARDINE OF SIENA

(1380–1444) Priest. Orphaned as a child, St. Bernadine was lovingly raised by an aunt. When a virulent plague broke out in 1400, he volunteered to care for the sick and only stopped when he succumbed to exhaustion. He joined the Franciscans and was ordained a priest in 1404. Finding that his true calling was to preach, he traveled all through present day Italy proclaiming the Gospel. So moved by the Holy Spirit, St. Bernadine once preached for fifty hours straight. He was canonized only six years after his death.

In all your actions see in the first place the Kingdom of God and his glory; persevere in brotherly charity, and practice first all that you desire to teach others.

—St. Bernardine of Siena

Jesus, Name full of glory, grace, love and strength! You are the refuge of those who repent, our banner of warfare in this life, the medicine of souls, the comfort of those who morn, the delight of those who believe, the light of those who preach the true faith, the wages of those who toil, the healing of the sick. To You our devotion aspires; by You our prayers are received; we delight in contemplating You. O Name of Jesus, You are the glory of all the saints for eternity. Amen.

—St. Bernardine of Siena

········

MAY 21

SAINT EUGENE DE MAZENOD

(1782–1861) Priest, bishop, founder. Born to a poor but aristocratic family, St. Eugene endured the chaos of the French Revolution and a poor family life before entering the seminary in 1805. As a priest he dedicated himself to helping the impoverished in Provence and founded the Missionary of Provence to minister to their needs. Later, he was named the Bishop of Marseilles and set about building churches and forming parishes. Later still he founded the Oblates of Mary Immaculate, missionaries who soon set sail to spread the Gospel to five continents. St. Eugene was canonized in 1995 by Pope John Paul II.

God our Father, we thank you for having
called Saint Eugene de Mazenod to follow
Christ the Savior and Evangelizer.
Through his intercession help us to reach out
with the healing touch of Christ who calls us
to holiness and to Mission.

May we be build communities which are signs of your
presence, and share the Good News of salvation
with all peoples.
For this we dedicate ourselves, through Christ our Lord.
Saint Eugene de Mazenod, Share with us your love for Christ.
Saint Eugene de Mazenod, Help us to stand firm in goodness.
Saint Eugene de Mazenod, Be with us in all our efforts
Amen.

—*Novena prayer to St. Eugene de Mazenod*

. . . .

MAY 22

SAINT RITA OF CASCIA

(1381–1457) Religious. St. Rita pleaded with her parents to let her join the convent, but they forced a marriage upon her instead. For close to twenty years she was married to a violent and abusive man. After her husband was murdered by an enemy and her two sons died of illness, St. Rita once again attempted to join a religious community. After several refusals because of her marriage, St. Rita was finally permitted to join the Augustinian nuns at Cascia. She lived a pious life of charity, prayer, penance, and fasting. Desiring to share in the Passion of Christ, her forehead was pierced as if by a thorn, which caused her great pain for the remainder of her life. St. Rita was canonized in 1900 by Pope Leo XIII. Like St. Jude, St. Rita is the patron of impossible cases.

Holy Patroness of those in need, Saint Rita, so humble, pure and patient, whose pleadings with thy Divine Spouse are irresistible, obtain for me from thy Crucified Christ my request. Be kind to me, for the greater glory of God, and I promise to honor thee and to sing thy praises forever.

Oh glorious St. Rita, who didst miraculously participate in the sorrowful Passion of our Lord Jesus Christ, obtain for me the grace to suffer with resignation the troubles of this life, and protect me in all my needs. Amen

—Prayer to St. Rita of Cascia

. . . .

MAY 23

SAINT JOHN BAPTIST ROSSI

(1698–1764) Priest. Born to a poor but pious family, St. John received a good education paid for by wealthy benefactors and felt a strong calling to the priesthood. Suffering from epilepsy, he required and received a special dispensation to become a priest. He devoted himself to the people of Rome and ministered tirelessly to them, most especially to homeless women, for whom he established a shelter, the sick, prisoners, and laborers. A zealous evangelizer, St. John was a great confessor and would preach many times a day wherever he could be heard—in prisons, barracks, chapels, hospitals, or churches. He gave away whatever money he earned to the poor, and when he finally died of a stroke, he was buried at the expense of the hospital where he had so often ministered to the sick. Known as "the apostle of the abandoned," St. John Baptist Rossi was canonized in 1881 by Pope Leo XIII.

Lord of the Harvest, bless young people with the gift of courage to respond to your call. Open their hearts to great ideals, to great things. Inspire all of your disciples to mutual love and giving—for vocations blossom in the good soil of faithful people. Instill those in religious life, parish ministries, and families with the confidence and grace to invite others to embrace the bold and noble path of a life consecrated to you. Unite us to Jesus through prayer and sacrament, so that we may cooperate with you in building your reign of mercy and truth, of justice and peace. Amen.

—Pope Francis, Prayer for Vocations

SAINT JOANNA

(died first century) Disciple. St. Joanna was the wife of King Herod's steward, Chuza. A close follower of Jesus, St. Joanna helped to provide for Jesus and the Apostles during Jesus' ministry. She was among the women who prepared Jesus' body after his death, and one of the women who found the empty tomb of Jesus on Easter morning.

Bless me, how great the philosophy of this woman to be counted worthy to be addressed also as one of the apostles!

—St. Chrysostom, speaking about St. Joanna

SAINT BEDE THE VENERABLE

(673–735) Monk, priest, and Doctor of the Church. Considered the most learned man of his times, St. Bede was raised and spent his entire life in Wearmouth Abbey. Both a Benedictine monk and a priest, St. Bede was a devout scholar whose writings cover a wide spectrum of knowledge, including history, philosophy, astronomy, music, and poetry. His seminal work is the *Ecclesiastical History of the English People* that meticulously details Britain's history from antiquity up through 731.

He alone loves the Creator perfectly who manifests a pure love for his neighbor.

—St. Bede the Venerable

On hearing Christ's voice, we open the door to receive Him, as it were, when we freely assent to His promptings and when we give ourselves over to doing what must be done. Christ, since He dwells in the hearts of His chosen ones through the grace of His love, enters so that He might eat with us and we with Him. He ever refreshes us by the light of His presence insofar as we progress in our devotion to and longing for the things of heaven. He Himself is delighted by such a pleasing banquet.

—St. Bede the Venerable, from his homily on the call of St. Matthew

....

MAY 26

SAINT PHILIP NERI

(1515–1595) St. Philip arrived in Rome as a teenager, studying philosophy and theology and tutoring the children of his landlord. Growing in wisdom and holiness, he founded the Confraternity of the Blessed Sacrament, aimed at helping the poor and the sick. At the age of thirty-five, he was ordained and found his mission space right on the streets of Rome. He became a great confessor and an esteemed spiritual director. Known as a saint who loved to laugh as well as to pray, St. Philip Neri is a saint for all ages.

Cheerfulness strengthens the heart and makes us persevere in the good life. Therefore the servant of God ought always to be in good spirits.

—St. Philip Neri

There is no more excellent way to obtain graces from God than to seek them through Mary, because her Divine Son cannot refuse her anything.

—St. Philip Neri

....

MAY 27

SAINT AUGUSTINE OF CANTERBURY

(died c. 606) Monk, evangelizer. A monk living a quiet, prayerful life as a prior at a monastery in Rome, St. Augustine was called by Pope Gregory the Great to journey to Anglo-Saxon England with thirty-nine monks to spread the Good News of the Gospel. A dangerous pursuit, St. Augustine deftly managed his task and won the permission of the king to preach and convert all who desired. The king himself was baptized in 597. Made the Bishop of Canterbury, he built a church and a monastery there and converted thousands of people in his eight years in England. The Good News that St. Augustine proclaimed would ultimately spread throughout all of the British Isles.

Your words are fair, but of doubtful meaning; I cannot forsake what I have so long believed. But as you have come from far we will not molest you; you may preach, and gain as many as you can to your religion.

—*King Ethelbert's greeting to St. Augustine upon the saint's arrival in England in 507*

. . . .

MAY 28

BLESSED MARGARET POLE

(1473–1541) Martyr. Born into English royalty, Blessed Margaret was the niece of King Edward IV and King Richard III. In 1491, she married Sir Reginald Pole and had five sons. After she was widowed, she was made a countess and governess to Princess Mary, the daughter of Henry VIII. When Blessed Margaret disapproved of King Henry's marriage to Anne Boleyn, she was exiled from court. She was later imprisoned, when her son, the future Cardinal Reginald Pole, challenged King Henry's Act of Supremacy. After being held in the Tower of London for two years, and never tried, Blessed Margaret was executed at the age of seventy. She was beatified in 1886.

For traitors on the block should die;
I am no traitor, no, not I!
My faithfulness stands fast and so,
Towards the block I shall not go!
Nor make one step, as you shall see;
Christ in Thy Mercy, save Thou me!

—*Inscribed on the wall of Blessed Margaret's cell, believed to be written by her*

BLESSED JOSEPH GERARD

(1831–1914) Priest, missionary. Blessed Joseph Gerard was born to French country people and joined the Missionary Oblates of Mary Immaculate at the age of twenty. At twenty-two he was sent to Southern Africa as a missionary— never again to return home or see his family. He spread the Good News to both the Zulu and Basotho peoples of South Africa. Taking care to learn their language and customs, Blessed Joseph was well received and later revered by the native people and the Oblate Mission flourished there. Lesotho is a predominately Catholic country today due in large part to the lifelong efforts of Blessed Joseph. Carrying on his work until his death at the age of eighty-three, Blessed Joseph was beatified by Pope John Paul II in 1988.

The secret of his holiness, the key to his joy and zeal, was the simple fact that he lived continually in the presence of God. Blessed Joseph's whole life was caught up in the love of the Holy Trinity. People wanted to be near to Father Gerard because he always seemed near to God. He was filled with a spirit of prayer, nourished daily by the Liturgy of the Hours and by frequent visits to the Blessed Sacrament. He had a fervent devotion to the Mother of God and the Saints. During his long and difficult journeys to outlying missions and the homes of the sick, he conversed continually with his beloved Lord. It is undoubtedly this vivid sense of being always in the presence of God that explains his lifelong fidelity to his religious vows of chastity, poverty and obedience and to his obligations as a priest.

—Pope John Paul II, homily at the beatification
of Blessed Joseph Gerard, September 1988

SAINT JOAN OF ARC

(1412–1431) Martyr. St. Joan of Arc was born to a devout peasant family in a remote village of France. From a young age, Joan heard the voices of the saints advising her. Upon such counsel, she convinced the crown prince of France to let her lead a small army against the English to help gain back French lands. Though Joan met with a series of military victories, she was finally captured by the English, tried, and convicted of heresy. She was famously burned at the stake on May 30, 1431. St. Joan of Arc was canonized in 1920 by Pope Benedict XV.

In the face of your enemies, in the face of harassment, ridicule, and doubt, you held firm in your faith. Even in your abandonment, alone and without friends, you held firm in your faith. Even as you faced your own mortality, you held firm in your faith. I pray that I may be as bold in my beliefs as you, St. Joan. I ask that you ride alongside me in my own battles.

Help me be mindful that what is worthwhile can be won when I persist. Help me hold firm in my faith. Help me believe in my ability to act well and wisely. Amen.

—*Prayer to St. Joan of Arc for faith*

THE VISITATION OF THE
BLESSED VIRGIN MARY

During those days Mary set out and traveled to the hill country in haste to a town of Judah, where she entered the house of Zechariah and greeted Elizabeth. When Elizabeth heard Mary's greeting, the infant leaped in her womb, and Elizabeth, filled with the holy Spirit, cried out in a loud voice and said, "Most blessed are you among women, and blessed is the fruit of your womb. And how does this happen to me, that the mother of my Lord should come to me? For at the moment the sound of your greeting reached my ears, the infant in my womb leaped for joy. Blessed are you who believed that what was spoken to you by the Lord would be fulfilled."

—Luke 1:39–45

I saw her ghostly, in bodily likeness: a simple maid and meek, young of age, and little waxen above a child, in the stature that she was when she conceived.

—Blessed Julian of Norwich about her vision of the Blessed Virgin

Him whom the heavens cannot contain, the womb of one woman bore. She ruled our Ruler; she carried Him in whom we are; she gave milk to our Bread.

—St. Augustine of Hippo

JUNE

SAINT JUSTIN

(c. 100–165) Martyr. Born to a pagan family in Palestine, St. Justin spent years studying philosophy and converted to Christianity at the age of thirty-three. From then on, he devoted his life to spreading the Good News throughout Asia Minor and in Rome and is known as the first Christian philosopher. While preaching he was arrested and ordered to renounce his faith. Refusing to do so, he was beheaded.

No right-minded man forsakes truth for falsehood.

—St. Justin's last words

To yield and give way to our passions is the lowest slavery, even as to rule over them is the only liberty.

—St. Justin

SAINT MARCELLINUS AND SAINT PETER

(died 304) Martyrs. Martyred during the reign of Diocletian, these holy men continued to spread the Gospel even after their imprisonment. They were taken to a remote wooded area and killed in secret. The truth about their faith and martyrdom was revealed however, as their executioner had become a Christian and proclaimed what he knew about these early saints.

Bless the martyrs heartily, that you may be a martyr by intention. Thus, even though you depart this life without persecutor, fire, or lash, you will still be found worthy of the same reward.

—St. Basil the Great

SAINT CHARLES LWANGA
AND COMPANIONS

(died 1886–1887) Martyrs. These martyrs from Uganda were killed during the reign of King Mwanga, a lustful tyrant who undertook violent persecutions against Christians beginning in 1885. When Joseph Mkasa, one of the king's subjects responsible for the court pages, spoke out against the king's wrongdoing, he was killed. St. Charles Lwanga rose up and tried to protect the court pages from the king's lust. The king was irate when he heard the young men were receiving instruction about Christianity. He ordered St. Charles and his companions to be wrapped in reed mats and burned alive. These martyrs were canonized in 1964 by Pope Paul VI. St. Charles Lwanga is the patron of African youth.

O Blessed St. Charles Lwanga and companions, you who faced evil, embraced the Good News, and died for your faith, pray for us!

SAINT FRANCIS CARACCIOLO

(1563–1607) Religious, founder. Born into a noble family, St. Francis contracted a leprosy-like illness in his youth. After a miraculous recovery, he dedicated himself to God. He was ordained and began ministering to prison inmates who were condemned to death. Later, he co-founded the Order of the Regular Clerics Minors, dedicated to the adoration of the Blessed Sacrament. He worked and suffered to expand the order until his death in 1607. St. Francis Caracciolo was canonized by Pope Pius VII in 1807.

Let us go, let us go to Heaven!

—*Last words of St. Francis Caracciolo*

SAINT BONIFACE

(c. 673–754) Monk, priest, bishop, martyr. Educated at a Benedictine monastery in England, he later became a monk, a teacher, and was ordained a priest. St. Boniface was sent as a missionary to Germany in 719. While he did not succeed on his first trip, he returned and boldly preached the Good News to all who would listen. As the bishop of Mainz, St. Boniface converted a great number of people and built many churches and monasteries. He was martyred by barbarians as he was preparing to confirm a group of converts. St. Boniface is the patron saint of Germany.

Let us be neither dogs that do not bark nor silent onlookers nor paid servants who run away before the wolf. Instead let us be careful shepherds watching over Christ's flock. Let us preach the whole of God's plan to the powerful and to the humble, to rich and to poor, to men of every rank and age, as far as God gives us the strength, in season and out of season.

—*St. Boniface*

SAINT NORBERT

(c. 1080–1134) Bishop. Born to a noble family, St. Norbert led an indulgent life in his youth but after he was thrown by his horse during a violent thunderstorm he experienced a spiritual awakening. He prepared for and was ordained to the priesthood and embarked on a life of preaching and penance. He was the founder of the Order of Premonstratensians and was made the archbishop of Magdeburg in Germany. St. Norbert was canonized in 1582 by Pope Gregory XIII.

O Priest! You are not yourself because you are God. You are not of yourself because you are the servant and minister of Christ. You are not your own because you are the spouse of the Church. You are not yourself because you are the mediator between God and man. You are not from yourself because you are nothing. What then are you? Nothing and everything. O Priest! Take care lest what was said to Christ on the cross be said to you: "He saved others, himself he cannot save!"

—*St. Norbert*

BLESSED ANNE OF SAINT BARTHOLOMEW

(1549–1626) Religious. Born to a peasant family in Spain and orphaned as a child, Blessed Anne spent years helping her brothers tend their sheep. Always possessed of a rich spiritual life, she experienced a vision with the Blessed Mother revealing to her that she would join a religious order. Blessed Anne became a lay sister with the Carmelites. She was a close friend and traveling companion of St. Teresa of Avila and held St. Teresa in her arms when she died. Thereafter, Blessed Anne worked tirelessly to establish additional Carmelite convents in France and the Netherlands.

Silence is precious; by keeping silence and knowing how to listen to God, the soul grows in wisdom and God teaches it what it cannot learn from men.

—*Blessed Anne of St. Bartholomew*

Mental prayer in my opinion is nothing else than an intimate sharing between friends; it means taking time frequently to be alone with Him who we know loves us.

—*St. Teresa of Avila*

JUNE 8

SAINT MELANIA THE ELDER

(325–410) Founder. Born to a noble family in Spain, St. Melania married young and moved to Rome with her husband and children. While in her twenties, she lost her husband and two of her three children and then converted to Christianity. She left for Alexandria to join the Christian ascetic movement and later embarked on a pilgrimage to the Holy Land where she founded a monastery on the Mount of Olives in Jerusalem. She went on to found additional monasteries and when she returned to Rome to visit her son, her granddaughter, also named Melania, followed her back to the Holy Land. Also a saint, her granddaughter is known as St. Melania the Younger.

Prayer was a continuous way of life in the desert. It was intentionally cultivated until it became second nature. Prayer involved the hard work of learning a new language—the language of heaven. For the ascetic, prayer was not merely the speaking of words. It was the heart yearning for God, reaching out in hopeful openness to being touched by God. Prayer was for the Holy Spirit breathing through the inner spirit of the ascetic and returning to God with yearnings of intimacy.
—The Forgotten Desert Mothers, *by Laura Swan*

....

JUNE 9

SAINT EPHREM

(c. 306–373) Deacon and Doctor of the Church. Banished from his pagan home for his Christian leanings, St. Ephrem was mentored by St. James, Bishop of Nisibis and was baptized at the age of eighteen. A fierce defender of the faith against heretics, he is known for his many spiritual writings and hymns. He penned so many hymns he came to be known as the "Harp of the Holy Spirit." He was made Doctor of the Church by Pope Benedict XV in 1920.

With the sign of the living cross, seal all your doings, my son. Don't go out the door of your house till you have signed the cross. Whether in eating or in drinking, whether in sleeping or in waking, whether in your house or on the road, or again in leisure hours, don't neglect this sign—for there is no guardian like it. It will be for you like a wall in the forefront of all you do.

—*St. Ephrem*

BLESSED HENRY OF TREVISO

(c. 1250–1315) Holy man. Born to a peasant family, Blessed Henry was uneducated but filled with love for God and neighbor. He worked as a day laborer to support his wife and child. After his wife and child died, he continued to work as a laborer but gave away his earnings to the poor. He was mocked for his physical appearance and his ragged clothes but was unfazed and continued to give all he had to the poor and homeless. Near the end of his life, when he could barely walk, he would drag himself to daily Mass. After his death, many miracles were ascribed to the intercession of this humble holy man.

The bread you store up belongs to the hungry; the cloak that lies in your chest belongs to the naked; the gold that you have hidden in the ground belongs to the poor.

—*St. Basil the Great*

SAINT BARNABAS

(died c. 61) Apostle, Martyr. A Jew born in Cyprus, his name was Joseph but he was given the name of Barnabas (meaning "son of encouragement") by the

Apostles, and was considered by them an Apostle though he was not one of the twelve. St. Barnabas is believed to have embraced Christianity shortly after Pentecost. He undertook many missionary journeys with St. Paul. He is referenced both in the Acts of the Apostles and in Paul's epistles. He is believed to have been martyred in Cyprus.

He was a good man, full of the Holy Spirit and faith, and a great number of people were brought to the Lord.

—*Acts of the Apostles 11:24, referring to St. Barnabas*

....

JUNE 12

SAINT JOHN OF SAHAGUN

(1419–1479) Priest, hermit. Born to a pious family, St. John was educated by the Benedictine monks. He was ordained and served faithfully as a parish priest, though he later felt called to the religious life and joined the Hermits of St. Augustine. A fearless preacher, confessor, and spiritual director, he may have been poisoned by one whose adulterous behavior he had denounced. He was canonized in 1690.

A preacher must be prepared in his soul to speak the truth, both in denouncing and correcting shortcomings and in praising virtue, to such a point that he is willing in that cause even to face death.

—*St. John of Sahagun*

....

JUNE 13

SAINT ANTHONY OF PADUA

(1195–1231) Priest and Doctor of the Church. Born to a noble family in Lisbon, he was inspired to join the Franciscans in 1220 and left for North Africa where

OPPOSITE: Saint Anthony of Padua

he earnestly desired martyrdom. His frail health however forced him to return to Italy. He grew into a fearless preacher and was known as the "hammer of the heretics." Blessed with mystical visions, he is famously known for miraculously holding the Christ child in his arms. St. Anthony is universally known as the saint to invoke when something is lost.

Among all things that are lovable, there is one that is more lovable than the rest, and that most lovable of all things is life.

—*St. Anthony of Padua*

The saints are like the stars. In His providence Christ conceals them in a hidden place that they may not shine before others when they might wish to do so. Yet they are always ready to exchange the quiet of contemplation for the works of mercy as soon as they perceive in their heart the invitation of Christ.

—*St. Anthony of Padua*

. . . .

JUNE 14

SAINT METHODIUS I

(died 847) Religious. Born into a wealthy Sicilian family, St. Methodius was highly educated and seeking a position at court when he heard God's call to the religious life. He rebuilt a monastery on the island of Chios and was later sent to Constantinople to combat the Iconoclast persecutions. He fervently defended the right of Christians to venerate sacred images. Imprisoned for seven years for his efforts, he was finally released and was elevated to the Patriarch of Constantinople.

To decorate their houses with religious pictures is a custom as old as Christianity itself, for the true Christian has always considered his home as nothing less than a temple of God, and the religious pictures as means to extend and preserve the spirit of Christianity in the home.

—*St. John Vianney*

SAINT GERMAINE OF PIBRAC

(1579–1601) Virgin. Born to a peasant family in France, St. Germaine's mother died when the future saint was only an infant. Her father remarried a cruel woman who abused and neglected St. Germaine. The girl suffered greatly at the hands of her stepmother and contracted disease from her maltreatment. With no one to turn to, St. Germaine turned to God and the Blessed Mother and found the solace in prayer that was denied to her in life. Her reputation for holiness grew and she died peacefully at the age of twenty-two. She is the patron of child abuse victims.

O Blessed Saint Germaine, who suffered abuse and neglect so patiently, look down from Heaven and intercede for the many abused children in our world. Strengthen and protect those children who have been abandoned by their parents and live on the streets. Let them know God's healing touch and help them find caregivers who will love and provide for them. Amen.

SAINT JOHN FRANCIS REGIS

(1597–1640) Priest. Descended from nobility in France, St. John Francis entered the Jesuit Order at the age of eighteen. After being ordained, he embarked on his work as a missionary preacher. He faced great hardship and privation on his missionary journeys but worked zealously to spread the Gospel. He was canonized in 1737 by Pope Clement XII.

I see Our Lord and his mother opening heaven for me.

—*Last words of St. John Francis Regis*

SAINT EMILY DE VIALAR

(b. 1797) Religious, founder. Born to a wealthy French family, St. Emily was educated in Paris but returned home to serve as a companion to her father after her mother died. She spent her days performing acts of charity for the sick and needy. Years later, upon inheriting a fortune at the death of her grandfather, St. Emily bought a large house and formed a new order with several other women, named the Sisters of St. Joseph of the Apparition. They devoted themselves to the care of the needy, the sick, and to the education of children. She oversaw her order for twenty-two years until her death.

Love one another.

—*St. Emily's last words to her sisters*

SAINT GREGORY BARBARIGO

(1625–1697) Priest, bishop, cardinal. Born to a respected Venetian family, St. Gregory was highly educated and embarked on a distinguished diplomatic career. Hearing God's call, he was ordained a priest and then made the first Bishop of Bergamo where he worked tirelessly to implement the reforms from the Council of Trent. Later named Bishop of Padua then Cardinal, he went on to found colleges, libraries, and seminaries. Known as a wise and understanding leader, he was beatified in 1761 and canonized in 1960 by Pope John XXIII.

O Blessed St. Gregory, you led your flock with wisdom and understanding. Help me to seek out God's wisdom in my life and to open my heart to that which I do not understand. I ask this in the name of Jesus Christ, our Lord and Savior. Amen.

SAINT ROMUALD

(c. 956–c. 1027) Religious. Living an aimless youth, St. Romuald witnessed his father kill a relative in a duel and he fled to the protection of a monastery, where he later became abbot. He founded several other monasteries and also founded the Order of the Camaldolese Bens. Facing false accusations and attempts on his life with patience and prayer, he died on June 19 in a monastery he had founded.

Take every opportunity you can to sing the Psalms in your heart and to understand them with your mind. And if your mind wanders as you read, do not give up; hurry back and apply your mind to the words once more. Realize above all that you are in God's presence, and stand there with the attitude of one who stands before the emperor. Empty yourself completely and sit waiting, content with the grace of God, like the chick who tastes nothing and eats nothing but what his mother brings him.

—*St. Romuald*

BLESSED MICHELINA

(1300–1356) Lay Franciscan. Born to a prosperous family, Blessed Michelina married the Duke of Malatesta when she was only twelve. By the age of twenty, she was a widow, and soon her only child died. Finding consolation in prayer, she desired to join the lay Franciscans. Her family was so furious, they had her locked away in an asylum. When she gained her release, she gave away her possessions and devoted her life to ministering to the sick, especially those afflicted with leprosy.

Everything people leave after them in this world is lost, but for their charity and almsgiving they will receive a reward from God.

—*St. Francis of Assisi*

Remember that the Christian life is one of action; not of speech and daydreams.

—St. Vincent Pallotti

SAINT ALOYSIUS GONZAGA

(1568–1591) Religious. Born into a family of wealth and prestige, St. Aloysius was expected to inherit his father's title of Marquis. Hearing God's call, he implored his parents to allow him to join the Society of Jesus. When plague broke out in Rome, he ministered to the sick until he caught the disease himself. He died six years short of being ordained as a Jesuit. He was canonized in 1726 and is the patron of youth.

I am going to heaven.

—St. Aloysius Gonzaga's last words

His call came before the first hour, when he was only a child. He used to tell me that he considered his seventh year to have been the year of his conversion. Then again, he never suffered from fleshly allurements, even in his thoughts, and he is the only one I know who was so singularly blessed. His third privilege was to be free of all distractions in his prayers, and how great a privilege that was, we who try to pray know best.

—St. Robert Bellarmine about St. Aloysius Gonzaga

SAINT THOMAS MORE

(1478–1535) Martyr. Trained as a lawyer, St. Thomas More was the Lord Chancellor of England and friend of King Henry VIII. He opposed the king's efforts to divorce Catherine of Aragon and marry Anne Boleyn. He was imprisoned and executed when he refused to sign the Act of Supremacy which declared the king the head of the Church in England. St. Thomas More is the patron saint of lawyers.

I die the King's good servant—but God's first.

—St. Thomas More's last recorded words, 1535

We may not look, at our pleasures, to go to heaven in featherbeds; it is not the way, for our Lord Himself went thither with great pain, and by many tribulations, which was the path wherein He walked thither, and the servant may not look to be in better case than his Master.

—St. Thomas More, to his wife and children

....
JUNE 23

SAINT JOSEPH CAFASSO

(1811–1860) Born to devout peasant parents, St. Joseph was sent to Turin to study for the priesthood and was ordained in 1833. After completing his education, he became a theology professor and lectured brilliantly on moral theology. Mentor and friend of St. John Bosco, St. Joseph was also known as a great confessor with a special dedication to the prison population of Turin. He was canonized by Pope Pius XII in 1947.

If you wish to walk securely and be certain of your salvation, if you aspire to a great crown in Heaven that will never fade, love and honor Mary, and strive to make her known, loved, and honored by others.

—St. Joseph Cafasso

I would be the happiest of men if I could become a saint soon and a big one.

—St. Joseph Cafasso

BIRTH OF SAINT JOHN THE BAPTIST

St. John the Baptist was the son of Zechariah and Elizabeth, who was the cousin of the Blessed Virgin Mary. The Gospels tell us that when Mary went to visit Elizabeth when Elizabeth was near the time of her son's birth, St. John "leapt in her womb." While he was still young, he went to the desert to live as a hermit and prepare himself for his ministry. It is believed he began his ministry at the age of thirty when he began to preach about the need for repentance for the coming of the Messiah. The Gospels tell us it was St. John who baptized Jesus. Falsely imprisoned and killed by King Herod, St. John the Baptist is considered the last prophet of the Old Testament.

No one can receive anything except what is given him from heaven. You yourselves bear me witness, that I said, I am not the Christ, but I have been sent before him. He who has the bride is the bridegroom; the friend of the bridegroom, who stands and hears him, rejoices greatly at the bridegroom's voice; therefore this joy of mine is now full. He must increase, but I must decrease.

—St. John the Baptist, John 3:27–30

Saint John appears as the boundary between the two Testaments . . . As representative of the past, he is born of aged parents; as a herald of the new era, he is declared to be a prophet while still in his mother's womb. For while yet unborn he leapt in his mother's womb at the arrival of the blessed Mary.

—St. Augustine of Hippo

SAINT EUROSIA (OR OROSIA) OF SPAIN

(d. 714) Martyr. It is said the Saint Eurosia was born to a noble family and was forced at the age of sixteen to marry a Moorish man in an arranged marriage

OPPOSITE: Saint John the Baptist

contrary to her Christian beliefs. She is said to have run off and hid in a cave to escape. The smoke from her fire gave her away, and she was dragged from the cave and martyred. She is the patron of Jaca, a city in northeastern Spain in the Pyrenees Mountains.

A fountain fed from many springs will never dry up. When we are gone, others will rise up in our place.

—*St. Bruno Serunkuma of Uganda*

....
JUNE 26

SAINT ANTHELM

(c. 1107–1178) Priest, monk, bishop. Born to a noble family, he heard God's call to serve and was ordained, joined the Carthusian monks, and was later made the Bishop of Belley. A great reformer and practical innovator, he rebuilt the monastery at Grand Chartreuse that had been nearly destroyed by an avalanche. He also put in place a network of aqueducts to provide fresh water for his people, and laid the foundation for the Carthusian Order to open a community for women. He spent his final years tending to the poor and sick.

O Blessed St. Anthelm, who worked tirelessly for the reforms that would improve the lives of your flock, help us to see where we need to reform our own lives. Help us to care for our neighbors, strive for holiness, and always follow the path that God has chosen for us. We ask this in the name of Jesus Christ our Lord. Amen.

....
JUNE 27

SAINT CYRIL OF ALEXANDRIA

(c. 376–444) Bishop and Doctor of the Church. Born in Alexandria, this bishop and theologian was a vigorous defender of the faith against the heresy that rejected the divine maternity of the Blessed Virgin. Though St. Cyril was successful in having the heresy condemned, he suffered many tribulations at the hands of heretics.

I have been amazed that some are utterly in doubt as to whether or not the Holy Virgin is able to be called the Mother of God. For if our Lord Jesus Christ is God, how should the Holy Virgin who bore him not be the Mother of God?

—*St. Cyril of Alexandria*

Assuredly, she who played the part of the Creator's servant and mother is in all strictness and truth in reality God's mother and lady and queen over all created things.

—*St. John of Damascus*

. . . .

JUNE 28

SAINT IRENAEUS OF LYONS

(second century) Priest, bishop. Known as one of the first great Catholic theologians, he was a follower of St. Polycarp, who in turn was a follower of St. John the Apostle. After studying in Rome, St. Irenaeus was ordained a priest and made the Bishop of Lyons. He made many missionary journeys and fervently defended the faith against the Gnostic heresy. He may have died a martyr's death.

It is not you that shapes God.
It is God that shapes you.
If then you are the work of God
await the hand of the artist who does
all things in due season.
Offer Him your heart,
soft and tractable,
and keep the form in which the artist

has fashioned you.
Let the clay be moist
lest you go hard
and lose the imprint of his Fingers.

—Prayer of St. Irenaeus

. . . .

JUNE 29

SAINT PETER AND SAINT PAUL

(died c. 64) Apostle. Saint Peter, named Simon at birth, was a Galilean fisherman. He left everything to follow Christ. St. Peter is referenced in the Gospels more than anyone, other than Christ. Jesus renamed him Peter, and foretold that Peter would be the "rock" upon which the Church would be built. After Jesus' Resurrection and Ascension, St. Peter became the first Pope. He led the fledgling Church for twenty-five years. Around the year 64, he was imprisoned and crucified upside down, believing himself to be unworthy to die as Christ did.

Blessed are you, Simon, son of Jonah. For Flesh and blood has not revealed this to you, but my heavenly Father. And so I say to you, you are Peter, and upon this rock I will build my church, and the gates of the netherworld shall not prevail against it. I will give you the keys to the kingdom of heaven. Whatever you bind on earth shall be bound in heaven; and whatever you loose on earth shall be loosed in heaven.

—Matthew 16:17–19

SAINT PAUL

(c. 5–c. 67) Apostle, martyr. A religious fanatic against the early Church, he was en route to Damascus to arrest Christians when he experienced a dramatic conversion to Christianity and became an Apostle. His writings have had a profound impact on the development of Christianity.

I want to know Christ and the power of his resurrection and the sharing of his sufferings by becoming like him in his death, if somehow I may attain the resurrection from the dead.

—St. Paul's Letter to the Philippians 3:8–11

. . . .

JUNE 30

THE FIRST MARTYRS
OF THE CHURCH OF ROME

In the year 64, there was a great fire in Rome that destroyed more than half of the city over a period of six days and seven nights. While it was rumored that Nero himself was responsible for the blaze, the blame was placed on the early Christians. Thousands of Christians were savagely murdered. It is believed that St. Peter and St. Paul were among the victims killed during this persecution.

Jesus answered them, "Take heed that no one leads you astray. For many will come in my name, saying, 'I am the Christ,' and they will lead many astray. And you will hear of wars and rumors of wars; see that you are not alarmed; for this must take place, but the end is not yet. For nation will rise against nation, and kingdom against kingdom, and there will be famines and earthquakes in various places: all this is but the beginning of the birth-pangs. Then they will deliver you up to tribulation, and put you to death; and you will be hated by all nations for my name's sake. And then many will fall away, and betray one another, and hate one another. And many false prophets will arise and lead many astray. And because wickedness is multiplied, most men's love will grow cold. But he who endures to the end will be saved."

—Matthew 24:4–13

JULY

....

JULY 1

BLESSED JUNIPERO SERRA

(1713–1784) Priest. Born in Petra, Spain, Blessed Juniper was a student at the Franciscan school and joined the Franciscan Order in 1730. He was ordained seven years later and spent years teaching theology and philosophy at the University of Padua. At the age of thirty-seven, he left on a missionary journey to "New Spain" (Mexico and California) and spent the remainder of his life working tirelessly to convert the native peoples there. He founded more than twenty missions and eventually six-thousand people were baptized into Christianity. A dedicated missionary beloved by his people, Blessed Juniper Serra was beatified by Pope John Paul II in 1988. Pope Francis has announced that he will canonize Blessed Juniper Serra on his visit to the United States in September of 2015.

All my life I have wanted to be a missioner. I have wanted to carry the Gospel teachings to those who have never heard of God and the kingdom He has prepared for them.

—*Blessed Junipero Serra*

JULY 2

BLESSED EUGENIA JOUBERT

(1876–1904). Religious. Born into a pious French family, Blessed Eugenia entered the Congregation of the Sisters of the Holy Family of the Heart of Jesus when she was nineteen. Possessed of a deep spiritual life and special connection to the Blessed Mother, she dedicated herself to teaching catechism especially to the children preparing for their First Holy Communion. Dying at the age of twenty-eight from tuberculosis, she was declared Blessed by Pope John Paul II in 1994.

You can do nothing with children unless you win their confidence and love by bringing them into touch with oneself, by breaking through all the hindrances that keep them at a distance. We must accommodate ourselves to their tastes, we must make ourselves like them.

—St. John Bosco

....

JULY 3

SAINT THOMAS THE APOSTLE

(died c. 72) Apostle. One of the twelve, St. Thomas was a beloved follower of Christ throughout his public ministry but is perhaps best known for doubting that Jesus had risen from the dead. Insisting that he would not believe until he put his fingers in Christ's wounds, Thomas was present eight days later when Christ appeared to the apostles and invited Thomas to do just that. Thomas did so and then professed his belief in the Resurrected Christ. Tradition holds that St. Thomas was sent to spread the Good News to various peoples and finally reached India where he was speared to death while spreading the faith.

Then He said to Thomas, "Reach here with your finger, and see My hands; and reach here your hand and put it into My side; and do not be unbelieving, but believing." Thomas answered and said to Him, "My Lord and my God!" Jesus said to him, "Because you have seen Me, have you believed? Blessed are they who did not see, and yet believed."

—John 20:27–29

....

JULY 4

SAINT ELIZABETH OF PORTUGAL

(c. 1271–1336) Lay Franciscan. Born a princess in Aragon, Spain, St. Elizabeth was given in marriage at the age of twelve to King Denis of Portugal and became the

Queen of Portugal as a teenager. Despite a difficult marriage and the infidelity of her husband, she lived piously, attended Mass daily, and devoted herself to many charitable activities, including founding homes for the poor, abandoned children, the sick, lepers, and troubled women; she also established a convent for the Poor Clare nuns. Known as a peacemaker both within her own family and among nations, St. Elizabeth continued her charitable work for eleven years after her husband died, moving to a residence near the St. Clare's convent which she had founded. She is the patron of difficult marriages, victims of adultery, and charitable workers.

O God, author of peace and lover of charity,
who adorned Saint Elizabeth of Portugal
with a marvelous grace for reconciling those in conflict,
grant, through her intercession,
that we may become peacemakers,
and so be called children of God.
Through our Lord Jesus Christ, your Son,
who lives and reigns with you in the unity of the Holy Spirit,
one God, for ever and ever. Amen.

—*Prayer honoring St. Elizabeth of Portugal*

. . . .
JULY 5

SAINT ANTHONY ZACCARIA

(1502–1539) Priest, founder. Born into a noble family, St. Anthony was drawn to the field of medicine and became a doctor at the age of twenty-two. He soon discovered however, that his true calling was to the religious life. After studying theology, he was ordained and later joined the Confraternity of Eternal Wisdom and devoted himself to performing acts of mercy. He later co-founded the Angelicals, a community dedicated to aiding women and girls who were being exploited and victimized. Later still, he founded the Order of Clerks Regular of St. Paul, dedicated to ministering to all those in need in Milan. After accomplishing so much for the Lord, he died at the age of thirty-seven. He was canonized in 1897 by Pope Leo XIII.

Spiritual life demands that you never turn back or stop going forward; but rather that, as soon as you taste it, you make progress day by day and, forgetting what lies behind, strain forward to what lies ahead.

—St. Anthony Zaccaria

Meditation on death keeps us from vice and spurs us to virtue. This kind of meditation is an encouragement to the wayward and a hope to the repentant.

—St. Anthony Zaccaria

········

JULY 6

SAINT MARIA GORETTI

(1890–1902). Martyr. A pious girl who lived with her widowed mother, St. Maria Goretti was fatally stabbed during an attempted rape. While she was dying in the hospital she forgave her murderer. Her attacker repented in prison and was present in the crowd when St. Maria was canonized in 1950 by Pope Pius XII. She is known as a patron of youth, purity, and of rape victims.

The value of Christian virtue is so great, so overwhelming, so imperative, that it is worth more than life. Purity is not just a separate part of our being. It belongs to our existence as a whole, it is essential for our life. Purity brings us in harmony of body and soul.

—Pope Paul VI, from his visit to the Shrine of St. Maria Goretti, September 1969

········

JULY 7

BLESSED ROGER DICKENSON, BLESSED RALPH MILNER, BLESSED LAWRENCE HUMPHREY

(died 1591) Marytrs. These English martyrs were victims of the persecution of

Catholics during the reign of Queen Elizabeth I. Blessed Roger Dickenson was an undercover priest; Blessed Ralph Milner was a Catholic convert, a husband, father, and farm laborer, and Blessed Lawrence Humphrey was a twenty-one year old convert. All three were tried and convicted of being Catholic. The judge took pity on Blessed Ralph Milner as he was the father of eight children. The judge told him if he simply went into a Protestant church for a few minutes his life would be spared. Mr. Milner refused and he and Father Dickenson went to their deaths followed by Blessed Lawrence.

The death of the martyrs blossoms in the faith of the living.

—St. Pope Gregory the Great

. . . .

JULY 8

BLESSED PETER THE HERMIT

(c. 1050–1115) Hermit, founder. Blessed Peter was living as a monk when he heard a rousing address from Pope Urban II urging Christians to join the crusades to reclaim the Holy Land. Heeding the pope's call, Blessed Peter traveled through Europe to zealously preach about the First Crusade. He then joined the First Crusade as a soldier and is said to have fought at Antioch and in the capture of Jerusalem in 1099. He returned thereafter and once again devoted himself to a spiritual life, founding a monastery where he lived out his years.

Christian warriors, He who gave His life for you, today demands yours in return. These are combats worthy of you, combats in which it is glorious to conquer and advantageous to die. Illustrious knights, generous defenders of the Cross, remember the example of your fathers who conquered Jerusalem, and whose names are inscribed in Heaven; abandon then the things that perish, to gather unfading palms, and conquer a Kingdom which has no end.

—St. Bernard of Clairvaux, preaching about the Second Crusades

ROSE HAWTHORNE, SERVANT OF GOD

(1851–1926) Founder. Daughter of American author Nathaniel Hawthorne, Rose married young to an editor of *The Atlantic Monthly*. Their only son died when he was five and both Rose and her husband moved to New York and converted to Catholicism. When her husband's struggles with alcoholism made it dangerous for Rose to stay with him, she made the difficult decision with the counsel of her priest to leave her husband who died a year later. In search of a new vocation, Rose moved to a tenement in the slums of New York City, took a nursing course, and opened a home for incurable cancer patients. At this time, it was a common belief that cancer was contagious, making Rose's dedication to helping cancer patients all the more laudable. Joining together with several other women, she founded the Dominican Congregation of St. Rose of Lima, later called the Servants of Relief for Incurable Cancer. In 1901, Rose, now known as Mother Alphonsa, opened Rosary Hill Home in Hawthorne, New York (now the mother home of the order). She died there July 9, 1926, after helping incurable impoverished cancer victims for thirty years. The Cause for the Beatification and Canonization of Rose Hawthorne (Mother Alphonsa) is currently underway.

I am trying to serve the poor as a servant. I wish to serve the cancerous poor because they are avoided more than any other class of sufferers; and I wish to go to them as a poor creature myself, though powerful to help through the open-handed gifts of public kindness, because it is by humility and sacrifice that we become worthy to feel the holy spirit of pity and to carry into the disorders of destitute sickness the cheerful love we have gathered from the Heavenly Kingdom for distribution.

—Rose Hawthorne, Servant of God

SAINT FELICITY AND HER SEVEN SONS

(second century) Martyrs. A noble Christian woman of Rome, St. Felicity, a widow, spent her days performing acts of charity and teaching others about Christ. Believing she was angering the gods, the pagan priests maligned her to the emperor who in turn had her arrested. Seven men, believed to be her sons, were arrested with her. When she refused to renounce her faith, even to spare the lives of her sons, she was forced to watch as each one was killed in front of her. Several months later she too was martyred.

I shall be beheaded. Within a few short hours my soul will quit this earth, exile over, and battle won. I shall mount upwards and enter into our true home. There among God's elect I shall gaze upon what eye of man cannot imagine, hear undreamed of harmonies, enjoy a happiness the heart cannot comprehend.

—*St. Theophane Venard*

SAINT DROSTAN

(died 610) Abbot. Born to a royal family in Ireland, St. Drostan was filled with sanctity at a young age and so was given to the care of St. Columba from whom he eventually accepted the habit. Together, they founded the monastery at Deir and when St. Columba left for Iona, St. Drostan stayed on as the abbot. Later, feeling drawn to a more secluded life of prayer, St. Drostan lived as a hermit where his piety drew many of the poor and needy to him.

O Blessed St. Drostan and faithful disciple of St. Columba, intercede for us that we may focus our lives on charity, prayer, and penance, that our souls may be saved. We ask this in the name of Jesus, our Lord and Savior. Amen.

SAINT JOHN GUALBERT

(died 1073) Monk, founder. Born into a noble family in Florence, St. John experienced a profound spiritual awakening while he was attempting to avenge his brother's death. On Good Friday, he happened upon his brother's murderer and was about to kill him when the man fell to his knees and begged mercy in the name of the crucified Christ. St. John was moved with pity for the man, put his sword away, and entered the nearest monastery church to repent for his sins. While there, he saw Christ bow his head from the cross. Such a conversion followed that St. John directly asked the abbot if he could join their order. He thus became a Benedictine monk but later left in search of a more austere community. He went on to found the Order of Vallombrosa, and did much to combat the vice of simony (the buying or selling for a price things of a spiritual nature) in his region. Serving the Lord until the age of eighty, he died peacefully and was canonized in 1193.

Look down upon me, good and gentle Jesus
while before Your face I humbly
kneel; and with burning soul pray and
beseech You to fix deep in my heart
lively sentiments of faith, hope, and charity;
true contrition for my sins, and a firm purpose
of amendment; while I contemplate,
with great love and tender pity
Your five wounds,
pondering upon them within me; while I
call to mind the words which David
Your prophet, said to You, my Jesus:
"They have pierced My hands and My feet,
they have numbered all My bones."

—Prayer Before a Crucifix

SAINT HENRY II

(972–1024) Emperor. Born in Bavaria, St. Henry was elected the emperor of Germany and then he and his wife, St. Cunegundes, were crowned emperor and empress of the Holy Roman Empire. He is said to have been miraculously cured by St. Benedict, and greatly desired to become a Benedictine himself. A just and compassionate ruler, St. Henry was declared a saint in 1146. He is the patron of the Benedictine Oblates.

O Blessed St. Henry, your strong faith helped you rule with justice and compassion. We pray that you will help us keep God at the center of our lives and help us find the courage to follow God's path for us whatever that may be. We ask this through Jesus Christ, our Lord and Savior. Amen.

BLESSED RICHARD LANGHORNE

(1624–1679) Martyr. An English martyr, Blessed Richard was educated at the Inner Temple and was a lawyer. He helped the Jesuits with legal and financial advice. Married to a Protestant woman, Blessed Richard's both sons were priests. Over the years, Blessed Richard was arrested and held in prison for long periods of time for trumped up charges. In the end, he was arrested in connection with the so-called "Popish Plot," sentenced to death and executed.

I am desirous to be with my Jesus. I am ready and you need stay no longer for me.

—Last words of Blessed Richard Langhorne

SAINT BONAVENTURE

(1221–1274) Bishop and Doctor of the Church. As a child, St. Bonaventure was cured by an illness through the intercession of St. Francis who himself gave the boy the name "Bonaventure." In his early twenties, St. Bonaventure moved to Paris and joined the Franciscan Order of Friars Minor where he taught theology. While studying in Paris, he became close friends with St. Thomas Aquinas and the two received their theology degrees together. When St. Bonaventure was thirty-five he was elevated to the General of the Friars Minor and was later made the Cardinal Archbishop of Albano. He was known as the leading Franciscan theologian and one of the greatest medieval philosophers in history, but also for his kindness, compassion, holiness, and gentleness. St. Bonaventure was canonized by Pope Sixtus IV in 1482.

No matter how much our interior progress is ordered, nothing will come of it unless by divine aid. Divine aid is available to those who seek it from their hearts, humbly and devoutly; and this means to sigh for it, in this valley of tears, through fervent prayer.

—*St. Bonaventure*

No angel, no saint, can equal her in the multitude and accumulation of heavenly good things.

—*St. Bonaventure, about the Blessed Mother*

OUR LADY OF MOUNT CARMEL

This is the feast of the Carmelites. The origin of this feast dates back to the twelfth century to the devout hermits who lived on Mount Carmel in northern Israel. It was there that these holy men dedicated the very first known chapel to the Blessed Virgin. They became known as the Brothers of Our Lady of Mount Carmel in the thirteenth century. In 1726 the universal Church began to celebrate this day as the Feast of Our Lady of Mount Carmel. Carmelites have always had a special bond with Mary.

O beautiful Fower of Carmel, most fruitful vine, Splendor of Heaven, holy and singular, who brought forth the Son of God, still ever remaining a Pure Virgin, assist me in this necessity. O Star of the sea, help and protect me! Show me that Thou art my mother.

—*from* The Flos Carmeli

In trial or difficulty I have recourse to Mother Mary, whose glance alone is enough to dissipate every fear.

—*St. Thérèse of Lisieux*

Pray especially to Our Blessed Mother Mary, placing all your intentions into her hands. For she loves you as she loves her Son. She will guide you in all your relationships so that peace may fill your life.

—*St. Thérèse of Lisieux*

· · · · · · · · ·

JULY 17

SAINT ALEXIS

(fifth century) Wandering holy man. The son of a Roman senator, St. Alexis was raised as a good Christian whose parents prevailed upon him to marry against his wishes. On his wedding day, he obtained permission from his bride to leave. He traveled to Syria and lived as a beggar, sharing what he had with other poor people. Thus he lived for seventeen years until his reputation for holiness drew others to him. He returned to Rome and to his family where he lived as a beggar—never telling his family his true identity. He was content to live under the stairs and spend his days in prayer and teaching the children about God. After his death, his family found a document on his person that confirmed that he was their lost son.

We have to serve God in His way, not in ours.

—*St. Thérèse of Lisieux*

Worldly people often purchase hell at a very dear price by sacrificing themselves to please the world.

—*Blessed Henry Suso*

· · · · · · · · ·
JULY 18

SAINT CAMILLUS DE LELLIS

(c. 1550–1614) Priest, founder. This Italian born saint, was a soldier with a severe gambling addiction. Penniless and with a diseased leg from a war injury, he turned to God. He attempted to join the Capuchin Order but his medical problems prevented his admission. After studying for the priesthood, he was ordained, and under the guidance of his confessor, St. Philip Neri, he was able to form his own order, the Ministers of the Sick or the Camellians. He and the others of his congregation devoted their lives to ministering to the sick—in hospitals, aboard plague ships, in the battle fields. Gravely ill for many years himself, he stepped down as the head of his order in 1607. St. Camillus was canonized in 1746 and is a patron of the sick, nurses, and hospitals.

The poor and sick are the heart of God. In serving them, we serve Jesus Christ.

—*St. Camillus de Lellis*

The true apostolic life consists in giving oneself no rest or repose.

—*St. Camillus de Lellis*

SAINT ARSENIUS

(c. 354–449) Monk. Born in Rome, he became a deacon and then tutor to the emperor of Constantinople's sons. He lived an ostentatious life of splendor for ten years before God called him to a simpler path. In or about 400, St. Aresenius joined the desert monks and lived a spare life of prayer, penance, and austerity. He died at the age ninety-five.

I have always something to repent for after having talked, but have never been sorry for having been silent.

—*St. Arsenius*

I know a great deal of Greek and Latin learning. I have still to learn even the alphabet of how to be a saint.

—*St. Arsenius*

SAINT APOLLINARIS

(died c. 200) Bishop, martyr. It is believed that St. Peter sent St. Apollinaris to Ravenna, Italy to serve as the first bishop there. While he was preaching the Good News there he was beaten by pagans and forced out of the city. Returning three subsequent times only to be driven out, he finally succumbed to his injuries.

We hope to suffer torment for the sake of our Lord Jesus Christ and so be saved.

—*St. Justin*

There are many among the martyrs of my age or younger, and as weak or weaker than I; but the Divine Grace that did not fail them will sustain me.

—*St. Robert Southwell*

SAINT LAWRENCE OF BRINDISI

(1559–1619) Priest and Doctor of the Church. Joining the Capuchin Franciscans at sixteen, St. Lawrence (born Julius Caesare Russo) traveled to Padua to study theology and learned six languages while he was there. After he was ordained a priest, he passionately spread the Good News as a missionary and converted many to Christianity. Armed with only a crucifix, he famously led troops into battle against the invading Turks. Known for his great holiness and wisdom, St. Lawrence was canonized in 1881 and made a Doctor of the Church in 1960.

The Holy Spirit sweetens the yoke of the divine law and lightens its weight, so that we may observe God's commandments with the greatest of ease and even with pleasure.

—St. Lawrence of Brindisi

SAINT MARY MAGDALENE

(first century) Disciple. A follower of Jesus throughout his public ministry, it is believed that St. Mary Magdalene was the first person to whom Jesus appeared to after his Resurrection. Others through history have identified her with the woman who washed Jesus' feet with oil after repenting of her sins.

The Magdalene, most of all, is the model I like to follow. That boldness of hers, which would be so amazing if it weren't the boldness of a lover, won the heart of Jesus, and how it fascinates mine!

—St. Thérèse of Lisieux

SAINT BRIDGET
(OR BIRGITTA) OF SWEDEN

(c. 1303–1373) Founder. The daughter of the Royal Prince of Sweden, St. Bridget had a special devotion to the Passion of Christ as a child. Obeying her father, she married a prince at the age of thirteen and bore eight children, including St. Catherine of Sweden. After the death of her husband, St. Bridget sought a life of piety. Renouncing her title, she founded the Order of the Most Holy Trinity or Brigettines. A known mystic, St. Bridget spent many years in Rome offering guidance and advice to popes and dignitaries alike.

The world would have peace if the men of politics would only follow the Gospels.

—St. Bridget of Sweden

The time will come when there will be one flock and one shepherd, one faith and one clear knowledge of God.

—St. Bridget of Sweden

SAINT DECLAN

(died fifth century) Priest, bishop. This early Irish saint spread the Good News in parts of Ireland prior to Saint Patrick. Baptized by and a disciple of St. Colman, he was a pious child who studied with holy men in Ireland and made several pilgrimages to Rome. He founded a monastery in Ardmore and was named the first Bishop of Ardmore. He died and was buried on the grounds of the monastery he founded. Many miracles have been attributed to his intercession, including the cessation of a deadly plague through his prayers and fasting.

He received marks of honour and sincere affection from the people and clergy of Rome when they came to understand how worthy he was, for he was comely, of good appearance, humble in act, sweet in speech, prudent in counsel, frank in conversation, virtuous in mien, generous in gifts, holy in life and resplendent in miracles.

—The Life of Saint Declan of Ardmore, edited and translated from
the twelfth century text by Rev. Patrick C. Power, 1914

·········

JULY 25

SAINT JAMES THE GREATER

(died 44) Apostle. One of the twelve, James the Greater was a fisherman like his father Zebedee and his brother John. He was fishing with his brother when Jesus passed and challenged them to become fishers of men. A close companion of Jesus, St. James was witness to many of the key events in the life of Jesus as recorded in the Gospels. While James was brash (he and his brother John were called "sons of thunder" by Jesus) James grew in wisdom and faith and fearlessly preached the Gospel after Jesus' Ascension. The first apostle to be martyred, James was put to death by King Herod Agrippa. He is the patron of laborers.

O Blessed St. James, because of your faith and fervor, Jesus chose you to witness the glory of His Transfiguration and His agony in Gethsemane. Obtain for us strength and consolation in the unceasing struggles of this life. We ask this in the name of Jesus Christ our Lord and Savior. Amen.

·········

JULY 26

SAINT JOACHIM AND SAINT ANN

Parents of Blessed Virgin Mary. Tradition holds that both St. Joachim and St. Ann hailed from the tribe of Judah of the house of David. It is traditionally held that St. Ann and St. Joachim were old and without children but implored God to bless them with a child. God heard their prayers and blessed them with Mary, the Blessed Virgin who would give birth to the Messiah. It is believed that they came from Galilee and settled in Jerusalem where Mary was born and raised. St. Ann is the patron saint of Christian mothers and women in labor. St. Joachim is the patron of grandparents.

Heavenly Father, You gave Saints Joachim and Ann the wonderful privilege of being the parents of the Virgin Mary and the grandparents of Christ, Your Son. Through their intercession bring us, our children, and our grandchildren closer to the loving Heart of Your Son, Who lives and reigns with You and the Holy Spirit, one God, forever and ever. Amen.

—Grandparents' Prayer

. . . .

JULY 27

SAINT PANTALEON

(c. 275–c. 303) Martyr. This early Christian was also a brilliant medical doctor—it is said that he was the personal physician of Emperor Galerius Maximian. He became so caught up in pagan affairs that St. Pantaleon lost his faith for a time. After listening to the wise counsel of a priest, he repented and regained his faith. He helped the sick and the needy, and gave away his possessions to the poor. During the Diocletian persecutions, St. Pantaleon was given the choice of renouncing his faith or death. Refusing to deny Christ, he was brutally tortured and killed.

O God, who bestowed upon St. Pantaleon the grace of exercising charity toward others by distributing his goods to the poor, and has made him a special patron of the sick, grant, that we, too, show our charity by works of mercy; and through the intercession of your holy saint that we are preserved from sickness. But if it be your will that illness should afflict us, give us the grace to bear it patiently, and let it promote our eternal salvation. Amen.

—*Prayer in honor of St. Pantaleon*

·········

JULY 28

SAINT BOTVID

(died c. 1120) Lay missionary, martyr of charity. Born to a pagan family in Sweden, St. Botvid learned about the Good News when trading in England. He converted to Christianity and traveled back to Sweden to proclaim Christ as a lay missionary. Desiring the Gospel to be preached in Finland too, St. Botvid acquired a slave and instructed in the faith. He set the man free to go back to Finland and evangelize. They set out in a boat for Finland, but the slave repaid St. Botvid by killing him in his sleep and stealing his boat. St. Botvid is known as a martyr of charity and is one of the apostles of Sweden.

O Blessed St. Bovid, you who spread the Good News of the Gospel throughout Sweden and died of martyr of charity, hear my prayers and obtain for me an answer to my petitions. Amen.

·········

JULY 29

SAINT MARTHA

(died c. 80) Disciple. The sister of Martha and Lazarus, St. Martha was a follower of Jesus who was visited by Jesus several times in her home over the course of his public ministry. The Gospels refer to her several times, including when she complains to Jesus that her sister isn't helping with the domestic work because she is attentively listening to Jesus. St. Martha is the patron of housewives, maids, servants, and cooks.

As Jesus and his disciples were on their way, he came to a village where a woman named Martha opened her home to him. She had a sister called Mary, who sat at the Lord's feet listening to what he said. But Martha was distracted by all the preparations that had to be made. She came to him and asked, "Lord, don't you care that my sister has left me to do the work by myself? Tell her to help me!"

"Martha, Martha," the Lord answered, "you are worried and upset about many things, but few things are needed—or indeed only one. Mary has chosen what is better, and it will not be taken away from her."

—Luke 10:38–42

· · · · · · · · ·

JULY 30

SAINT PETER CHRYSOLOGUS

(406–c. 450) Bishop and Doctor of the Church. Born in Italy, he was mentored and educated under the guidance of the Bishop of Imola. He lived for a monk for many years but was called to be Bishop of Ravenna. He ruled his flock with compassion and care and was known for his gifted oratory. St. Peter Chrysologus was named a Doctor of the Church in 1729.

Mildness overcomes anger, meekness extinguishes fury, goodness coaxes malice away, affection lays cruelty low, patience is the scourge of impatience, gentle words vanquish quarrelsomeness, and humility prostrates pride.

—St. Peter Chrysologus

SAINT IGNATIUS OF LOYOLA

(1491–1556) Priest, founder. Born into a noble family in Spain, St. Ignatius was "given over to the vanities of the world" in his youth. When he was wounded in battle, he spent months bedridden during his convalescence. After reading and reflecting on the life of Christ and of the saints, he experienced a deep spiritual awakening. He changed his name to Ignatius, lived for a time as a hermit, and studied Latin and philosophy. He and several companions founded a new order—the Society of Jesus or Jesuits. He was General of the Society for more than fifteen years and by the time of his death there were one thousand Jesuits. St. Ignatius Loyola died peacefully and was canonized by Pope Gregory XV in 1622.

It is true that the voice of God, having once fully penetrated the heart, becomes strong as the tempest and loud as the thunder; but before reaching the heart it is as weak as a light breath which scarcely agitates the air. It shrinks from noise, and is silent amid agitation.

—St. Ignatius of Loyola

Everything that one turns in the direction of God is a prayer.

—St. Ignatius of Loyola

In a time of desolation, never forsake the good resolutions you made in better times. Strive to remain patient—a virtue contrary to the troubles that harass you—and remember that you will be consoled.

—St. Ignatius of Loyola

Take, O Lord, and receive my entire liberty, my memory, my understanding and my whole will. All that I am and all that I possess You have given me. I surrender it all to You to be disposed of accordingly to Your will. Give me only Your love and Your grace; with these I will be rich enough and will desire nothing more.

—*Prayer of St. Ignatius of Loyola*

OPPOSITE: Saint Ignatius of Loyola

AUGUST

AUGUST 1

SAINT ALPHONSUS LIGOURI

(1696–1787) Bishop and Doctor of the Church. Born near Naples, St. Alphonsus was filled with piety as a child. Possessed of a keen intellect, he finished his legal studies at the age of sixteen. He soon discovered his true calling was from God and was ordained a priest in 1726. He later founded the Congregation of the Most Holy Redeemer or Redemptorists whose focus was to preach to the poor and working class people. He was made Bishop of St. Agatha and lovingly led his flock for almost twenty years. A prolific writer, he penned more than sixty books over the course of his lifetime. He endured great physical suffering during the last years of his life and was crippled, deaf, and nearly blind at his death. After faithfully serving God for more than sixty years, he died at happy death. St. Alphonsus Ligouri was canonized in 1839 and made a Doctor of the Church in 1871.

God wills only our good; God loves us more than anybody else can or does love us. His will is that no one should lose his soul, that everyone should save and sanctify his soul. . . . God has made the attainment of our happiness, His glory. Even chastisements come to us, not to crush us, but to make us mend our ways and save our souls.

—*St. Alphonsus Ligouri*

If you embrace all things in life as coming from the hands of God, and even embrace death to fulfill His holy will, assuredly you will die a saint.

—*St. Alphonsus Ligouri*

BLESSED JANE OF AZA

(1135–1205) Mother of St. Dominic. Born to a noble family in Spain, Blessed Jane married young and bore several children. When she was pregnant with Dominic, her last son, she had a vision that foretold the profound role he would play in the Church. She lovingly cared for her family and devoted herself to acts of charity for the poor and needy. Three of her sons heard God's call to the priesthood. Antonio became a secular priest; Manez a Friar Preacher who was later beatified; and Dominic, the brilliant founder of the Dominicans and one of the most beloved saints in history. A saintly woman whose living example of faith inspired her sons to dedicate themselves to God, Blessed Jane was beatified in 1828.

Almighty God, who made known to your servant, Blessed Jane, the grace of the heavenly calling of her son, Dominic, we beseech You that by imitating her and her son we may by their loving intercession receive everlasting rewards. We ask this through Jesus Christ our Lord. Amen.

SAINT LYDIA

(first century) Born in Thyatira in Asia Minor, a place well known for its dye works, St. Lydia was St. Paul's first convert to Christianity in Philippi. Baptized together with the others in her household, she asked Paul and his companions to stay and visit at her house.

A certain woman named Lydia, a seller of purple, of the city of Thyatira, one who worshiped God, heard us; whose heart the Lord opened to listen to the things which were spoken by Paul. When she and her household were baptized, she begged us, saying, "If you have

judged me to be faithful to the Lord, come into my house, and stay."
So she persuaded us.

—Acts of the Apostles 16:14–15

AUGUST 4

SAINT JOHN VIANNEY

(1786–1859) Born to a family of devout peasants in France, St. John ardently desired to become a priest but had much difficulty in his studies for the priesthood. He was finally ordained when he was almost thirty years old and assigned as a parish priest at the unassuming parish of Ars where he stayed for more than forty years. In time, his sanctity and virtue attracted pilgrims from all over the world to see the humble saint. A brilliant confessor and reader of souls, he was known to hear confessions for up to sixteen hours a day. Beloved for his simplicity and gentleness, St. John Vianney was canonized by Pope Pius XI in 1925. He is the patron of parish priests.

The more we know of men, the less we love them. It is the contrary with God; the more we know of Him, the more we love Him.

—St. John Vianney

Love of our neighbor consists of three things: to desire the greater good of everyone; to do what good we can when we can; to bear, excuse, and hide other's faults.

—St. John Vianney

· · · · · · · · · · ·

AUGUST 5

BLESSED FREDERIC JANSSOONE

(1838–1916) Religious. The youngest of thirteen children born to a wealthy Flemish farming family in France, he lost his father when he was nine and helped his mother by selling things door to door. At twenty-three, his mother died and he found himself drawn to the religious life. He joined the Franciscans and was ordained in 1870 thus beginning a long life of varied service for the Lord. He spent time as a military chaplain during the Franco-Prussian War, made multiple journeys to the Holy Land on various missions, and finally moved to Canada where he spent more than twenty years. During his time there, he reestablished the Third Order of Saint Francis and did much to establish a shrine to Our Lady at Cap-de-la-Madeleine in Quebec. Known as a joyful and faith-filled preacher, Blessed Frederic was beatified by Pope John Paul II in 1988.

O Blessed Frederic Janssoone, you who joyfully spread the Gospel of the Lord in the Holy Land, help us to be joyful in our lives and to spread the Word of God in the spirit of St. Francis through our actions as well as our words. We ask this in the name of Jesus Christ, our Lord and Savior. Amen.

....

AUGUST 6

THE TRANSFIGURATION OF THE LORD

From the cloud came a Voice that said, "This is
My Son, the Beloved; listen to Him!"

—*Luke 9:35*

In the event of the Transfiguration we contemplate the mysterious encounter between history, which is being built every day, and the blessed inheritance that awaits us in heaven in full union with Christ, the Alpha and the Omega, the Beginning and the End. We, pilgrims on earth, are granted to rejoice in the company of the transfigured Lord when we immerse ourselves in the things of above through prayer and the celebration of the divine mysteries. But, like the disciples, we too must descend from Tabor into daily life where human events challenge our faith. On the mountain we saw; on the paths of life we are asked tirelessly to proclaim the Gospel which illuminates the steps of believers.

—*Pope John Paul II, August 6, 1999*

· · · · · · · · · · ·

AUGUST 7

SAINT CAJETAN

(1480–1547) Priest. Born to a noble family in Vincenza, Italy, St. Cajetan studied law and worked in the papal offices of Rome. He was later ordained a priest and devoted himself to helping the poor and the sick in his native city. Later, he founded the Order of the Theatines, a community of priests who preached the Gospels in the spirit of the Apostles. Always concerned with helping the poor, he founded a bank that would cater to them which later became the Bank of Naples. The patron of the unemployed, St. Cajetan was canonized in 1671.

Do not receive Christ in the Blessed Sacrament so that you may use Him as you judge best, but give yourself to Him and let Him receive you in this Sacrament, so that He Himself, God your Savior, may do to you and through you whatever He wills.

—*St. Cajetan*

· · · · · · · · · · ·

AUGUST 8

SAINT DOMINIC

(c. 1170–1221) Born into a noble family in Spain, St. Dominic studied for seven years with a maternal uncle who was a priest and then studied for ten years at Palencia, both the arts and theology. When St. Dominic finished his studies, he took the habit of the Regular Canons of St. Augustine and devoted his time to preaching, prayer, and works of charity. Though serious and scholarly, he was filled with compassion for the poor and was eager to relieve their suffering.

Tradition holds that he twice attempted to sell himself into slavery to obtain the funds to free others. When he accompanied his bishop on a missionary journey to France, his life took a dramatic turn. It was there that he was exposed to the virulent heresies that were tearing at the fabric of the Church and he knew that he was being called by God to vigorously defend the faith. To better preach the truth of the Gospel, St. Dominic founded the Order of the Dominicans. He chose the cities of Paris and Bologna to teach and train his brothers and then sent them out two by two on their preaching missions. At the time of his death, the Dominicans were thriving throughout all of Europe. A brilliant and faith-filled leader, St. Dominc was canonized in 1234.

A man who governs his passions is master of the world. We must either command them, or be enslaved by them. It is better to be a hammer than an anvil.

—St. Dominic

Arm yourself with prayer instead of a sword; be clothed with humility instead of fine raiment.

—St. Dominic

You are my companion and must walk with me. For if we hold together no earthly power can withstand us.

—St. Dominic, upon meeting St. Francis

....

AUGUST 9

SAINT EDITH STEIN (TERESA BENEDICTA OF THE CROSS)

(1891–1942) Religious, martyr. The eleventh child born into a devout Jewish family in Germany, St. Edith was a scholarly child. Her father died when she was two years old and her mother was left to raise the children alone. By the time she was a teenager, St. Edith had lost her Jewish faith and considered herself an atheist. It was her studies in philosophy that led her to Christianity.

After fortuitously reading the autobiography of St. Teresa of Avila, St. Edith was ready to embrace Christianity and was baptized in 1922. Very active in the Catholic Women's Movement in Germany, she was a prominent writer, teacher, and lecturer, and was well known in the academic world by the time Hitler rose to power. In 1933, she fulfilled her long held desire to join a religious order. She joined the Carmelites and became Sister Teresa Benedicta of the Cross. After five years in Cologne, she and her sister who had also joined the order were sent to a Carmelite convent in Holland for their protection. After Holland fell to the Nazis, St. Edith and her sister Rose were rounded up and sent to Auschwitz on August 2, 1942. Eyewitnesses from the death camp recall St. Edith as possessing a great inner strength and caring for the other prisoners, especially the children during the brief time she was there. She and her sister were executed on August 9, 1942. St. Edith Stein was canonized on October 11, 1998 by Pope John Paul II.

God is there in these moments of rest and can give us in a single instant exactly what we need. Then the rest of the day can take its course, under the same effort and strain, perhaps, but in peace. And when night comes, and you look back over the day and see how fragmentary everything has been, and how much you planned that has gone undone, and all the reasons you have to be embarrassed and ashamed: just take everything exactly as it is, put it in God's hands and leave it with Him. Then you will be able to rest in Him—really rest—and start the next day as a new life.

—St. Edith Stein

We cannot separate love for God from love for man. We acknowledge God easily, but our brother? Those with whom we do not identify in his background, education, race, complexion. We could not have imagined that love for God could be so hard.

—St. Edith Stein

OPPOSITE: Saint Edith Stein

SAINT LAWRENCE

(died 258) Deacon, martyr. Born in Spain, this early martyr was one of seven deacons of the early Church charged with helping those in need. During the Christian persecutions under Emperor Valerian, Pope St. Sixtus II was condemned to death and instructed St. Lawrence to distribute the Church's possessions to the poor. When St. Lawrence refused to hand over the Church's treasures to the Roman prefect but instead presented him with the poor, he was likewise sent to his death. Praying till his last breath for the conversion of Rome, several senators who witnessed St. Lawrence's brutal death are said to have embraced Christianity thereafter.

Learn, unhappy man, how great is the power of my God; for your burning coals give me refreshment, but they will be your eternal punishment. I call Thee, O Lord, to witness: when I was accused, I did not deny Thee; when I was questioned, I confessed Thee, O Christ; on the red-hot coals I gave Thee thanks. . . .

—St. Lawrence at his martyrdom

SAINT CLARE OF ASSISI

(1194–1253) Religious, founder. Born into a noble family in Assisi, Italy, St. Clare heard St. Francis preach and was so deeply moved that she ran away to join him. The group of sisters that she founded under his guidance was the Poor Clares or the Second Order of St. Francis. Her mother and two sisters eventually joined her. Led by St. Clare, the mortifications and austerities practiced by the Poor Clares were legendary—including wearing no shoes, sleeping on the ground, and living in absolute poverty. Second to St. Francis alone, she is responsible for the proliferation of the Franciscans. St. Clare was canonized in 1255, only two years after her death.

Our labor here is brief, but the reward is eternal. Do not be disturbed by the clamor of the world, which passes like a shadow. Do not let the false delights of a deceptive world deceive you.

—*St. Clare of Assisi*

Go forth in peace, for you have followed the good road. Go forth without fear, for He who created you has made you holy, has always protected you, and loves you as a mother. Blessed be you, my God, for having created me.

—*St. Clare, uttered to herself on her deathbed*

AUGUST 12

SAINT JANE FRANCES DE CHANTAL

(1572–1641) Founder. Born in Dijon, France, she married a baron at the age of twenty-two and bore six children, three of whom died. A widow eight years later, she did the best she could to provide for her children. She met St. Frances de Sales and he became her spiritual director. Though she felt a strong calling to the religious life, he persuaded her to postpone joining a community. Under his guidance, she later founded the Order of the Visitation of Our Lady, an order for women desiring the religious life who because of frail health, their age, or other considerations were barred from other religious communities. Extolling the virtues of meekness and humility, the sisters of the new community focused on performing spiritual and corporal works of mercy. St. Jane faced many struggles and temptations and endured long periods of spiritual dryness—yet she persevered and achieved sainthood in 1767.

She was full of faith, yet all her life had been tormented by thoughts against it. While apparently enjoying the peace and easiness of mind of souls who have reached a high state of virtue, she suffered such interior trials that she often told me her mind was so filled with all sorts of temptations and abominations that she had to strive not to look within herself. . . . But for all that suffering her face never lost its serenity, nor did she once relax in the fidelity God asked of her. And so I regard her as one of the holiest souls I have ever met on this earth.

—St. Vincent de Paul about St. Jane Frances de Chantal

AUGUST 13

SAINT BENILDUS

(1805–1862) Religious. Born to a French farming family, this member of the Christian Brothers taught students for more than forty years. He was responsible for developing progressive teaching methods such as positive reinforcement to motivate students rather than punishments. Beatified in 1948 by Pope Pius XII, he was lauded for achieving his sanctity through enduring the "terrible daily grind." Displaying the patience of a saint with his students, St. Benildus was canonized in 1969 by Pope Paul VI.

I imagine that the angels themselves, if they came down as schoolmasters, would find it hard to control their anger. Only with the help of the Blessed Virgin do I keep from murdering some of them.

—St. Benildus

AUGUST 14

SAINT MAXIMILIAN KOLBE

(1894–1941) Priest, martyr. Born in Poland, Saint Maximilian joined the Franciscans and was ordained a priest in 1918. He founded the Militia of Immaculate Mary which sought to bring about conversion through the absolute dedication to the Blessed Mother. A vocal opponent of the Nazis, he was sent to a concentration camp during World War II. He offered his life in exchange for a married man with a child who was about to be killed for helping an escaped prisoner. He died of starvation in August of 1941. St. Maximilian Kolbe was canonized in 1982.

OPPOSITE: Saint Maximilian Kolbe

Never be afraid of loving the Blessed Virgin too much. You can never love her more than Jesus did.

—St. Maximilian Kolbe

The most deadly poison of our times is indifference. And this happens, although the praise of God should know no limits. Let us strive, therefore, to praise Him to the greatest extent of our powers.

—St. Maximilian Kolbe

．．．．．．．．．．．．

AUGUST 15

THE ASSUMPTION OF THE BLESSED VIRGIN

We pronounce, declare and define it to be a divinely revealed dogma that the immaculate Mother of God, the ever Virgin Mary, having completed the course of her earthly life, was assumed body and soul to heavenly glory.

—Pope Pius XII, *declaring the Assumption of Mary as a dogma of faith, November 1, 1950*

As the most glorious Mother of Christ, our Savior and our God and the giver of life and immortality, has been endowed with life by him, she has received an eternal incorruptibility of the body together with him who has raised her up from the tomb and has taken her up to himself in a way known only to him.

—St. Modestus of Jerusalem

Who could believe that God would repay His Mother for elements of His human Body, by allowing the flesh and blood from which it was taken to decay in the grave?

—Blessed John Henry Cardinal Newman

SAINT STEPHEN OF HUNGARY

(c. 969–1038) Catholic king. A Christian from the age of ten, St. Stephen (known as Vaik prior to his baptism) became the first Catholic king of Hungary. He was deeply committed to the Church and to serving the poor. He led his largely pagan people to the Church through the intercession of the Blessed Mother. Known to dress in disguise so he could anonymously give alms to the poor, St. Stephen ruled Hungary with wisdom and charity for more than forty years. He was canonized, along with his son, by Pope St. Gregory VII in 1083. St. Stephen is the patron saint of Hungary.

Be merciful to all who are suffering violence, keeping always in your heart the example of the Lord who said, "I desire mercy and not sacrifice."

—*St. Stephen of Hungary*

SAINT CLARE OF MONTEFALCO

(c. 1268–1308) Born in Italy, St. Clare was called to the religious life as a young woman and joined the Franciscan tertiaries. She and her companions established the Holy Cross Convent in 1290 under the Rule of St. Augustine. She succeeded her sister as the abbess of the community and devoted herself to prayer and severe penance and had a special devotion to the Passion of Christ. One of the incorruptibles, St. Clare was canonized in 1881 by Pope Leo XIII.

Who teaches the soul, if not God? There is no better instruction for life than that which comes from God. If God did not protect me, I would be the greatest sinner in the world.

—*St. Clare*

SAINT HELENA OF THE CROSS

(first century). Born to humble parents in Asia Minor, she married a Roman general and bore the son who would become Constantine the Great. She was divorced by her husband for another woman, but upon his death, her son Constantine conferred on her the title of Augusta. She and her son came to embrace Christianity and Constantine put in place and later expanded the Edict of Milan, granting Christians the right to freely worship thus ending three-hundred years of persecution. Sent by her son on a pilgrimage to Jerusalem, tradition holds that St. Helena inquired and searched tirelessly until she was finally able to locate the Cross of Christ. It is said that she was responsible for building eighty churches in the Holy Land.

Holy and blessed Saint Helena, with the anguish and devotion with which you sought the Cross of Christ, I plead that you give me God's grace to suffer in patience the labors of this life, so that through them and through your intercession and protection, I will be able to seek and carry the Cross, which God has placed upon me, so that I can serve Him in this life and enjoy His Glory ever after. Amen.

—*A Prayer to St. Helena*

SAINT JOHN EUDES

(1601–1680) Priest, founder. Born to a family of French farmers, St. John joined the Order of the Oratorians and was ordained a priest at the age of twenty-four. He then traveled through France as a missionary, preaching the Gospels with a passion that led to many conversions. He later founded the Congregation of the Priests of Jesus and Mary and the Sisters of Our Lady of Charity. His devotion to the Sacred Heart of Jesus and the Immaculate Heart of Mary prompted Pope Pius XI to name him the father of the cults of the Hearts of Jesus and Mary.

OPPOSITE: Saint Helena of the Cross

Finally, you are one with Jesus as the body is one with the head. You must, then, have one breath with Him, one soul, one life, one will, one mind, one heart. And He must be your breath, heart, love, life, your all.

—St. John Eudes

Give thanks to Almighty God who resists the proud and gives grace to the humble, and offer Him all the glory that this Maiden accorded to His majesty by her practice of the richest humility during her childhood and throughout the rest of her life.

—St. John Eudes

· · · · · · · · · · · · ·

AUGUST 20

SAINT BERNARD OF CLAIRVAUX

Just as Mary surpassed in grace all others on earth, so also in heaven is her glory unique. If eye has not seen or ear heard or the human heart conceived what God has prepared for those who love Him {1 Cor 2:9}, who can express what He has prepared for the woman who gave Him birth and who loved Him, as everyone knows, more than anyone else?

—St. Bernard of Clairvaux

In dangers, doubts, and difficulties, call upon Mary. Let her name be on your lips, and always in your heart. So that you may secure the assistance of her prayers, do no neglect to walk in her footsteps.

—St. Bernard of Clairvaux

The saints have no need of honor from us; neither does our devotion add the slightest thing to what is theirs. Clearly, if we venerate their memory, it serves us, not them. But I tell you, when I think of them, I feel myself inflamed by tremendous yearning.

—St. Bernard of Clairvaux

SAINT PIUS X

(1835–1914) Born into a very poor family in Italy, he was a responsible and scholarly child who would walk miles to school barefoot so to save his one pair of good shoes. St. Pius became a priest and was devoted to caring for the poor for seventeen years. His allegiance to the poor never wavered even as he was elevated to bishop and cardinal. His pontificate began in 1903. Possessing a special devotion to the Holy Eucharist, he lowered the age for First Communion to seven years old and encouraged his flock to receive the Eucharist as often as possible. A vigorous leader of the Church known for his liturgical reforms, battles against heresies and political extremism, Pope Saint Pius X was canonized by Pope Pius XII in 1954.

Holy Communion is the shortest and safest way to heaven. There are others: innocence, but that is for little children; penance, but we are afraid of it; generous endurance of trials of life, but when they come we weep and ask to be spared. The surest, easiest, shortest way is the Eucharist.

—St. Pius X

I was born poor, I have lived in poverty, and I wish to die poor.

—St. Pius X

THE QUEENSHIP OF MARY

Let all, therefore, try to approach with greater trust the throne of grace and mercy of our Queen and Mother, and beg for strength in adversity, light in darkness, consolation in sorrow; above all let them strive to free themselves from the slavery of sin and offer an unceasing homage, filled with filial loyalty, to their Queenly Mother. Let her churches be thronged by the faithful, her feast-days honored; may the beads of the Rosary be in the hands of all; may

Christians gather, in small numbers and large, to sing her praises in churches, in homes, in hospitals, in prisons.

—from the Encyclical of Pope Pius XII on Proclaiming the Queenship of Mary, October 11, 1954

. . . .

AUGUST 23

SAINT ROSE OF LIMA

(1586–1617) Born in Lima, Peru to Spanish parents, St. Rose embraced her call to the religious life and sought to model herself after St. Catherine of Siena. As such, she entered the Dominicans as a tertiary but did so in a shack in the garden of her home as there were no convents in Peru. Possessed of a deeply mystical prayer life, she practiced severe mortifications and cared for the poor and sick especially among the slave and Indian populations. St. Rose was the first person to be declared a saint from the Americas.

Without the burden of afflictions it is impossible to reach the height of grace. The gifts of grace increases as the struggles increase.

—St. Rose of Lima

. . . .

AUGUST 24

SAINT BARTHOLOMEW

(first century) Apostle, martyr. One of the twelve, St. Bartholomew (known as Nathaniel in the Gospel of John) was a faithful follower of Christ who Christ described as one in "whom there was no guile." After the Ascension, tradition holds that he preached in India and Turkey and Armenia where he was flayed alive and then crucified.

O Glorious St. Bartholomew, Jesus called you a person without guile and you saw in this word a sign that he was the Son of God and King of Israel. Obtain for us the grace to be ever guileless and innocent as doves. At the same time, help us to have your gift of faith to see the Divine hand in the events of daily life. May we discern the signs of the times that lead to Jesus on earth and will eventually unite us to him forever in heaven.

—*Prayer honoring St. Bartholomew*

. . . .

AUGUST 25

SAINT JOSEPH CALASANZ

(1556–1648) Priest, founder. This Spanish saint was the youngest of five children. After the deaths of his brother and mother he heard God's call to the religious life—he studied for and was ordained to the priesthood. He traveled to Rome as assistant to a cardinal and was dismayed at the plight of the poor in Rome. He established a number of schools for the impoverished children of Rome, thus laying the foundations for the Order of Clerks Regular of the Poor Schools of the Mother of God. He was canonized in 1767 by Pope Clement XIII and in 1948 Pope Pius XII declared him the "celestial patron of all the Christian popular schools."

In deep silence and peace of body and soul, kneeling down or choosing any other convenient posture, following Saint Paul's example, we will strive to contemplate Christ crucified and His virtues, so as to know and imitate them, so that we can remember them during the whole day

—*St. Joseph Calasanz*

SAINT ELIZABETH BICHIER DES AGES

(1773–1838) Founder. Born into a noble family in France, St. Elizabeth's family lost everything in the French Revolution. An intelligent woman, St. Elizabeth studied law and took her family's case to court and won. Following her dream of a religious life, she founded, with the help of St. Andrew Fournet, a new order called the Daughters of the Cross, which focused on caring for the sick and the aged and teaching children. She worked tirelessly to promote the new community and by 1830 sixty convents of the Daughters of the Cross had been established. The last years of her life were marred by continual illness and suffering but this woman of faith and action continued her work until she died peacefully in 1838. St. Elizabeth was canonized in 1947 by Pope Pius XII.

O Blessed St. Elizabeth Bichier des Ages, who did much to spread the faith and minister to the needy after the dark days of the French Revolution, intercede for us that we may face the challenges of our lives with courage and rely on God to sustain us when we sink into despair. We ask this in the name of Jesus Christ our Lord. Amen.

SAINT MONICA

(332–387) Mother of St. Augustine. St. Monica was raised as a good Christian but married a pagan who was very bad tempered towards her. She prayed endlessly for him to reform his ways and turn to God. On his deathbed he finally embraced Christianity, as did his mother. Her sufferings increased with her son's self-indulgent lifestyle and his heretical beliefs. She prayed fervently for his conversion and was thrilled that he returned to Christ and was baptized on Easter Eve by St. Ambrose. Having completed her life's mission, St. Monica died the following year.

For my part, my son, I no longer find pleasure in anything that this life holds. What I am doing here still, or why I am still here, I do not know, for worldly hope has withered away for me. One thing only there was for which I desired to linger in this life: to see you a Catholic Christian before I died. And my God has granted this to me more lavishly than I could have hoped, letting me see even you spurning earthly happiness to be His servant. What am I still doing here?

—St. Monica, as quoted by St. Augustine from his Confessions

. . . .
AUGUST 28

SAINT AUGUSTINE OF HIPPO

(354–430) Bishop of Doctor of the Church. This African-born saint was reared as a Christian by his mother St. Monica, but was tempted by worldly offerings and even espoused heretical beliefs until he finally accepted Christ at his baptism by St. Ambrose in 386. He was ordained and made the Bishop of Hippo. He worked zealously until the end of his life writing, preaching, and leading his flock. A brilliant propagator of the faith, and the greatest of the Latin Fathers of the Church, St. Augustine died in 430.

Restless are our hearts until they rest in Thee. All abundance which is not from God to me is neediness. This, then, is the full satisfaction of souls, this is the happy life: to recognize piously and completely the One through Whom you are led into the truth, the nature of the truth you enjoy, and the bond that connects you with the supreme measure.

—St. Augustine of Hippo

Do not grieve or complain that you were born in a time when you can no longer see God in the flesh. He did not in fact take this privilege from you. As He says: "Whatever you have done to the least of my brothers, you did to me."

—St. Augustine of Hippo

BEHEADING OF
SAINT JOHN THE BAPTIST

As for me, I baptize you with water; but One is coming who is mightier than I, and I am not fit to untie the thong of His sandals; He will baptize you with the Holy Spirit and fire. {Luke 3:16}

—*St. John the Baptist*

Celebrating the martyrdom of St John the Baptist reminds us too, Christians of this time, that with love for Christ, for his words and for the Truth, we cannot stoop to compromises. The Truth is Truth; there are no compromises. Christian life demands, so to speak, the "martyrdom" of daily fidelity to the Gospel, the courage, that is, to let Christ grow within us and let him be the One who guides our thought and our actions.

—*Pope Benedict XVI, August 29, 2012*

AUGUST 30

SAINT MARGARET WARD
AND BLESSED JOHN ROCHE

(died 1588) Martyrs. St. Margaret Ward was a lady's companion during the reign of Queen Elizabeth I. She contrived a plan to help an imprisoned priest, Father Richard Watson, escape from prison. When the boatman she'd hired to help her backed out, her servant Blessed John Roche, helped Father Watson gain his freedom. Both St. Margaret and Blessed John were arrested and tortured and both refused to reveal the location of Father Watson. Offered a pardon if they would renounce their faith, they refused, and were executed.. St. Margaret was beatified in 1929 and canonized in 1970 and Blessed John was beatified in 1929.

OPPOSITE: Saint Augustine of Hippo

The martyrs desired death, not to fly labor, but to attain their goal. And why do they not fear death, from which man naturally shrinks? Because they had vanquished the natural love of their own bodies by divine and supernatural love.

—St. Catherine of Siena

············

AUGUST 31

SAINT AIDAN OF LINDISFARNE

(died 651) Religious, founder. This Irish saint became a monk on the Island of Iona in Scotland and was later sent to Northumbria on a missionary journey. Once there, he established a monastery on the island of Lindisfarne and was made bishop. He and his companions devoted themselves to spreading the Gospel to all who would listen. Known for his sanctity, gentleness, and kindness to the poor and animals, St. Aidan is considered one of the Apostles of Northumbria.

He neither sought nor loved anything of this world, but delighted in distributing immediately to the poor whatever was given him by kings or rich men. He traversed both town and country on foot, never on horseback, unless compelled by some urgent necessity. Wherever on his way he saw any, either rich or poor, he invited them, if pagans, to embrace the mystery of the faith; or if they were believers, he sought to strengthen them in their faith and stir them up by words and actions to alms and good works.

—Venerable Bede about St. Aidan of Lindisfarne

SEPTEMBER

. . . .

SEPTEMBER 1

SAINT GILES

(died c. 724) Hermit. St. Giles was born in Athens, Greece of noble heritage. It is believed that he lost his parents as a young man and used the fortune they left him to help the poor and needy. As his reputation for holiness and charity grew, he left Greece for France to avoid the great admiration he was receiving in his homeland. In France, the gentle saint spent years living as a hermit and devoted his life to prayer. He was revered by the French king who eventually built a large monastery in honor of the saint. St. Giles gathered some disciples and presided there as abbot. Greatly venerated in the Middle Ages, St. Giles is the patron of many things including crippled people, nursing mothers, and night terrors.

O God, we beseech You to grant us through the merits and intercession of St. Giles to flee from the vanity and praise of this world, to avoid carefully all occasions of sin, to cleanse our hearts from all wickedness by a sincere confession, to leave this world in Your love and rich in good works, and to find You gracious on the day of judgment. We ask this through Christ our Lord. Amen.

—*Prayer in honor of St. Giles*

. . . .

SEPTEMBER 2

SAINT INGRID OF SWEDEN

(died 1282) Religious. Born to a noble family in Sweden, St. Ingrid was a pious woman who came under the spiritual direction of a Dominican monk, Father Peter of Dacia. Under his direction, she became the first Dominican nun in Sweden and founded the first Dominican cloister there. She died in 1282 of natural causes and miracles were obtained through her intercession.

The canonization process for her was begun in 1405, but the findings were inconclusive. Her cause was reopened in 1497 and her relics were translated (moved from one place to another in a solemn ceremony allowing for local veneration of the holy person) but the formal canonization seems not to have occurred. Her relics and cloister were destroyed during the Reformation.

O Blessed St. Ingrid, you who became the first Dominican nun in all of Sweden, pray for us that through your intercession and through the intercession of St. Dominic, we may obtain the blessings which we seek and obtain eternal salvation in heaven. We ask this in the name of Jesus Christ our Lord and Savior. Amen.

. . . .

SEPTEMBER 3

SAINT GREGORY THE GREAT

(c. 540–604) Pope and Doctor of the Church. Saint Gregory the Great was born into a wealthy aristocratic family in Rome. He finished his legal studies and rose through the secular ranks to become the prefect of Rome while he was still a young man. After five years, he resigned his worldly position in order to devote his life to God. He joined the Benedictine monks and founded six monasteries. In 590, he reluctantly accepted the papacy at the age of fifty. During the course of his pontificate, he managed to reform the clergy and the liturgy, exhausted the papal treasury to help the needy, and expanded the role and increased the strength of the papacy. Known as the "father of the medieval papacy," St. Gregory the Great is widely considered the greatest pope in the history of the Church.

For the soul is the inner face of man, by which we are known, that we may be regarded with love by our maker.

—*St. Gregory the Great*

Those who stumble on plain ground should shrink from approaching a precipice.

—*St. Gregory the Great*

The disbelief of Thomas has done more for our faith than the faith of the other disciples. As he touches Christ and is won over to belief, every doubt is case aside and our faith is strengthened.

—St. Gregory the Great

. . . .

SEPTEMBER 4

SAINT ROSALIA

(died c. 1160) Virgin, hermit. Born in Palermo, Sicily to a family descended from Charlemagne, St. Rosalia left her life of luxury in favor of dwelling in a cave and conversing only in prayer. She died alone around 1160 and was canonized by Pope Urban VIII in 1625. She is the patron of Palermo and invoked against the plague as her intercession halted the spread of a deadly plague in Palermo in 1624.

I, Rosalia, daughter of Sinibald, Lord of Roses and Quisquina, have taken the resolution to live in this cave for the love of my Lord, Jesus Christ.

—St. Rosalia, words she scrawled into the cave where she lived as a hermit

. . . .

SEPTEMBER 5

BLESSED TERESA OF CALCUTTA

(1910–1997) Religious, founder. Born Agnes Gonxha Bojaxhiu, she was the youngest of three children born to devout Catholic parents of Albanian descent. A happy child who was very involved in church activities, Agnes began to realize she had a religious vocation at the age of twelve. In 1928, she joined the Sisters of Our Lady of Loreto, an Irish order that ran missionary schools in India. After two years as a novice, she made her temporary vows and chose the name of Teresa. For seventeen years Blessed Teresa lived in Calcutta and taught at a high school for middle-class girls. It was in 1946, however, that she heard God calling her to a different vocation. After prayerful consideration, she made the difficult decision to leave her order to help the poorest of the poor in the slums of Calcutta. Some

of her former students joined her and in 1950 the Order of Missionaries of Charity was authorized by the pope. In 1952, she opened a home for the dying and the next year her first orphanage. Her order has spread to more than 130 countries running a vast network of shelters, clinics, and hospices. Mother Teresa died at the age of eighty-seven, after serving the poorest of the poor for five decades. She was beatified on October 19, 2003 by Pope John Paul II.

Prayer is not asking. Prayer is putting oneself in the hands of God, at His disposition, and listening to His voice in the depths of our hearts.
—*Blessed Teresa of Calcutta*

Love is not patronizing and charity isn't about pity, it is about love. Charity and love are the same—with charity you give love, so don't just give money but reach out your hand instead.
—*Blessed Teresa of Calcutta*

Let us ask Our Lady, in a very special way: Mary, mother of Jesus, be a mother to each of us, that we, like you, may be pure in heart, that we, like you, love Jesus; that we, like you, serve the poorest for we are all poor. First let us love our neighbors and so fulfill God's desire that we become carriers of his love and compassion.
—*Blessed Teresa of Calcutta*

SEPTEMBER 6

BLESSED BERTRAND OF GARRIGUES

(died 1230) Religious. Born in the south of France, Blessed Bertrand was educated by the Cistercian nuns. Desiring to devote his life to God, he was ordained a secular priest and joined the Cistercian missionaries who were seeking to defend the faith against the Albigensian heresy that was spreading at the time.

OPPOSITE: Blessed Teresa of Calcutta

This heresy perceived the physical world as evil and only the spiritual world as God's domain. The Church moved vigorously to stamp out this heresy, including a crusade in 1209 ordered by Pope Innocent III. Searching for a peaceful means to defend the faith, Blessed Bertrand found a kindred spirit in St. Dominic. Joining St. Dominic, Blessed Bertrand became one of the six preachers who formed the heart of the newly formed Order of Preachers or Dominicans. He was later appointed as the Prior Provincial of one of the eight provinces of the Dominican Order and spent the last nine years of his life preaching the true faith in southern France, where he founded the well known Priory of Marseille. The holy friar died at the age of thirty-five, having accomplished much for the Lord in his short life. He was declared Blessed by Pope Leo XIII in 1881.

O Blessed Bertrand, you who defended the faith through peaceful means and were a devoted follower and dear friend of St. Dominic, grant that through your loving intercession, we may follow in your footsteps and always endeavor to defend the faith while seeking to gain an understanding and tolerance for the faith of others. We ask this through Christ our Lord. Amen.

. . . .

SEPTEMBER 7

SAINT CLOUD (OR CLODOALD)

(c. 524–c. 560) A descendent of King Clovis, the first Christian king of the Franks, St. Cloud was raised with his brothers by his grandmother, St. Clothilde. Desiring the throne, a wicked uncle attempted to kill St. Cloud and his brothers. Though his brothers were killed, St. Cloud escaped and spent the rest of his life as a hermit, devoting himself to prayer, charity, penance, and preaching.

O Blessed St. Cloud, you who renounced worldly treasures and titles to devote your life to the Lord in prayer, give me through your intercession the strength to reject the empty promises of this world and to set my sights upon gaining our Father's Heavenly Kingdom. I ask this in the name of Jesus Christ, our Lord and Savior. Amen.

THE NATIVITY OF THE
BLESSED VIRGIN MARY

The birth of the Blessed Virgin has been celebrated in the Church since the sixth century or earlier. The September date was chosen because that is the beginning of the liturgical year for the Eastern Church where the celebration originated. The September 8th date is exactly nine months after the feast of the Immaculate Conception. Tradition in the Church is that Mary's parents, St. Ann and St. Joachim were an older couple without child who fervently prayed to God for the blessing of a child. Mary was delivered unto them, destined to be the Mother of God.

The Son of God became man for our salvation but only in Mary and through Mary.

—St. Louis Marie de Montfort

Today the Virgin is born, tended and formed and prepared for her role as Mother of God, who is the universal King of the ages.

—St. Andrew of Crete

She is the flower of the field from whom bloomed the precious lily of the valley. Through her birth the nature inherited from our first parents is changed.

—St. Augustine of Hippo

To give worthy praise to the Lord's mercy, we unite ourselves with Your Immaculate Mother, for then our hymn will be more pleasing to You, because she is chosen from among men and angels. Through her, as through a pure crystal, Your mercy was passed on to us. Through her, man became pleasing to God; Through her, streams of grace flowed down upon us.

—St. Faustina

SAINT PETER CLAVER

(1580–1654) Priest. St. Peter was born in Spain and educated in Barcelona. Heeding God's call to a life of missionary work, he joined the Jesuits and left his home in 1610, never to return. He journeyed to South America, to the center of the African slave trade, and was ordained there in 1615. He devoted the next forty years to ministering to the slaves and providing for their physical and spiritual needs. He gave whatever he could to ease their suffering—bread, medicine, lemons, brandy, and tobacco—and taught them about Christianity with the aid of pictures and interpreters. It is said that St. Peter baptized more than 300,000 slaves during his ministry. At the age of seventy, he was so ill with tremors that he could no longer continue his ministry. After four years of intense pain, suffering, and neglect, St. Peter died. He was canonized in 1888 by Pope Leo XIII who declared him the patron of all missionary work among black people.

To love God as He ought to be loved, we must be detached from all temporal love. We must love nothing but Him, or if we love anything else, we must love it only for His sake.

—*St. Peter Claver*

If being a saint consists in having no taste and a strong stomach, I admit I may be one.

—*St. Peter Claver*

SAINT NICHOLAS OF TOLENTINO

(1245–1305) Born in Italy, he joined the Augustinian friars and devoted himself to preaching and helping the poor and abandoned. Later ordained a priest, he spent the last thirty years of his life tirelessly ministering to the people of Tolentino. Though he suffered with many painful ailments throughout his life, he died a happy death in 1305 and was canonized in 1446. He is the patron of souls in purgatory.

O God of infinite goodness, through the prayers of St. Nicholas of Tolentino, we come before You with great confidence on behalf of the Holy Souls in Purgatory. In Your great mercy, free them from any stain of sin and bring them into Your heavenly kingdom. We ask this through the name of Jesus Christ, our Lord and Savior. Amen.

SAINT JOHN GABRIEL PERBOYRE

(1802–1840) Religious, martyr. Born in France to a large, pious family, St. John Gabriel heard God's call while he was accompanying his brother to the seminary. He thus joined the Vincentians and was ordained in 1825. He taught theology and rose through the ranks of his order with various positions until he heard God calling him once again, this time to undertake missionary work in China. He arrived there in 1835, spent time learning the language, and devoted himself to helping forgotten and abandoned children. In 1839, the persecutions against Christians began. After being arrested, tried, and tortured, the saint was strangled on a cross on September 11, 1840. Beatified by Pope Leo XIII in 1889, St. John Gabriel became the first martyr in China to be beatified. He was canonized in 1996 by Pope John Paul II..

I do not know what awaits me in the journey that lies ahead of me, without a doubt the cross, which is the daily bread of the missionary. What we can hope for better, going to preach a crucified God?

—St. John Gabriel Perboyre, letter written at the gateway to China

THE MOST HOLY NAME OF MARY

The feast to honor the Holy Name of Mary was deemed a universal feast of the Church by Pope Innocent XI on September 12, 1683.

In dangers, in hardship, in every doubt, think of Mary, call out to Mary. Keep her in your mouth; keep her in your heart. Follow the example of her life and you will obtain the favor of her prayers. Following her, you will never go astray. Asking her help, you will never despair. Keeping her in your thoughts, you will never wander away. With your hand in hers, you will never stumble. With her protection you will not be afraid. With her leading you, you will never tire. Her kindness will see you through to the end. Then you will know by your own experience how true it is that the Virgin's name is Mary.

—St. Bernard of Clairvaux

SAINT JOHN CHRYSOSTOM

(c. 350–407) Bishop and Doctor of the Church. Born in Antioch to devout Christian parents, he lived as a hermit in the mountains for six years after the death of his mother. Forced to return to Antioch due to illness, he was made a deacon, ordained a priest, and evolved into a fiery and eloquent preacher. Made Bishop of Constantinople, he was an outspoken critic of the rich and powerful and was driven into exile on several occasions. Finally exiled to the furthest reaches of the empire, his body gave out and he met his heavenly reward. He is the patron of preachers.

Do you want to honor Christ's body? Then do not scorn Him in his nakedness, nor honor Him here in the Church with silken garments while neglecting Him outside where He is cold and naked. The rich man is not one who is in possession of much, but one who gives much.

—St. John Chrysostom

. . . .

SEPTEMBER 14

THE EXALTATION OF THE CROSS

It is believed that the Holy Cross upon which Jesus was crucified was hidden to prevent his followers from obtaining it. Tradition holds that St. Helena located the True Cross in Jerusalem in 326. To commemorate this momentous event, her son, Constantine the Great ordered the erection of churches at the place of the Holy Sepulcher and on Mount Calvary. In 614, the king of Persia invaded Jerusalem and stole the relic of the True Cross. The emperor of Constantinople and his army forced the Persians to return holy relic wherein the emperor himself is said to have carried the Cross up Calvary to return it to the Church of the Holy Sepulcher in 629. The feast of the Exaltation or Triumph of the Cross was first celebrated in Jerusalem but was celebrated by the universal Church by about 720. The feast is a triumphant liturgy and a reminder that the Cross is the symbol of our salvation.

Whoever doesn't seek the cross of Christ doesn't seek the glory of Christ.

—St. John of the Cross

Be proud that you are helping God to bear the Cross, and don't grasp at comforts. It is only mercenaries who expect to be paid by the day. Serve Him without pay.

—St. Teresa of Avila

It's true, I suffer a great deal—but do I suffer well? That is the question.

—St. Thérèse de Lisieux

OUR LADY OF SORROWS

The feast of Our Lady of Sorrows was granted by Pope Pius VII in 1814. The Seven Sorrows of Mary are the Prophecy of Simeon; the Flight into Egypt; the Loss of Jesus in the temple; the Meeting of Jesus and Mary on the Way of the Cross; Mary at the Foot of the Cross; Jesus Taken down from the Cross; the Burial of Jesus.

Behold, this child is set for the fall and rising of many in Israel, and for a sign that is spoken against (and a sword will pierce through your own soul also), that the thoughts of many hearts may be revealed.

—Luke 2:35

The Virgin Mary, who believed in the word of the Lord, did not lose her faith in God when she saw her Son rejected, abused and crucified. Rather she remained beside Jesus, suffering and praying, until the end. And she saw the radiant dawn of His Resurrection. Let us learn from her to witness to our faith with a life of humble service, ready to personally pay the price of staying faithful to the Gospel of love and truth, certain that nothing that we do will be lost.

—Pope Benedict XVI, Angelus, September 13, 2009

SAINT CORNELIUS
AND SAINT CYPRIAN

(3rd Century) Pope, Bishop, martyrs. St. Cornelius was the pope, elected in 251. His papacy was challenged but he later garnered the support of sixty bishops and moved forward as the lawful pope. St. Cyprian was the bishop of Carthage and a supporter of St. Cornelius, the two shared faith-filled correspondence despite the chaotic events surrounding them. St. Cornelius died in exile in 253 under the persecution ordered by Emperor Gallus. St. Cyprian, who had faithfully led his flock for ten years, was martyred in 258 under the persecutions of Emperor Valerian.

When we pray, we pray not for one person but for all, because we are all one. God, the Master of peace and harmony, desires that we should pray for all even as He Himself bore us all.

—*St. Cyprian*

. . . .

SEPTEMBER 17

SAINT ROBERT BELLARMINE

(1542–1621) Bishop and Doctor of the Church. Born in to a large family in Tuscany, Italy, St. Robert was educated by the Jesuits and joined the Society of Jesus in 1560. A brilliant scholar and preacher, St. Robert was a staunch defender of the faith against Protestantism and a central figure during the Counter Reformation. He was elevated to a cardinal but still he adhered to his austere lifestyle and performed many charitable works. St. Robert was canonized and named a Doctor of the Church in 1930.

Peace and union are the most necessary of all things for men who live in common, and nothing serves so well to establish and maintain them as the forebearing charity whereby we put up with another's defects. There is no one who has not his faults, and who is not in some way a burden to others, whether he be a superior or a subject, an old man or a young, a scholar or a dunce.

—*St. Robert Bellarmine*

SAINT JOSEPH OF COPERTINO

(1603–1663) Priest. Born to a poor family in Copertino, Italy. He was a humble stable boy for the Franciscans. He joined the order in 1625 and was ordained a priest in 1628. So mystical was his prayer life that he was known to experience spiritual ecstasies and levitations. Plagued with suspicions, trials, and temptations, he bore it all with humility and patience. Canonized by Pope Clement XIII in 1767, he is the patron of air, space travelers, and students studying for exams.

O Great St. Joseph of Cupertino, your humble devotion and simplicity earned you a shower of blessings on earth, grant that through your intercession, I may receive the blessings which I seek and gain my eternal reward in Heaven. I ask this through Christ our Lord. Amen.

SAINT GENNARO (JANUARIUS)

(c. 275–c. 305) Bishop, martyr. Born in the area of Naples or Benevento, he was made bishop and was brutally martyred during the persecutions under Emperor Diocletian. It is said that the saint was mauled by bears in an amphitheater and then beheaded. His blood was later brought back to Naples. The blood has liquefied in its container from time to time dating back for six centuries. Most recently, the blood partially liquefied when Pope Francis held the relic in which the blood was contained and kissed it. Prior to that, the blood had not liquefied during a papal presence since 1848.

The bishop just announced that the blood half-liquefied. We can see the saint only half loves us. If only half of it liquefied that means we still have work to do; we have to do better. We must all spread the Word, so that he loves us more!

—Pope Francis, Cathedral of Naples, March 21, 2015

SAINT ANDREW KIM TAEGON AND SAINT PAUL CHONG HASANG AND COMPANIONS

Martyrs. St. Andrew Kim Taegon was born in 1881 to Christian parents. He studied in China where he was ordained a priest by the French missionaries. In secret, he returned to Korea where he was discovered, arrested, and beheaded in 1848. St. Paul Chong Hasang was a devout Christian who witnessed his father and brother die for their Christian faith. He was likewise arrested and shared their fate in 1839. Together with another 101 Korean martyrs, St. Andrew and St. Paul were canonized in 1984 by Pope John Paul II from the Seoul Cathedral. In August of 2014, Pope Francis beatified an additional 124 Korean Catholics who were martyred for their faith.

Today we celebrate this victory in Paul Yun Ji-chung and his 123 companions. Their names now stand alongside those of the holy martyrs Andrew Kim Taegon, Paul Chong Hasang and companions. . . . All of them lived and died for Christ, and now they reign with him in joy and in glory. With Saint Paul, they tell us that, in the death and resurrection of his Son, God has granted us the greatest victory of all. For "neither death, nor life, nor angels, nor principalities, nor things present, nor things to come, nor powers, nor height, nor depth, nor anything else in all creation, will be able to separate us from the love of God in Christ Jesus our Lord" (Romans 8:38–39).

—Pope Francis, August 16, 2014

SEPTEMBER 21

SAINT MATTHEW

(first century) Apostle and evangelist. One of the twelve, St. Matthew (known as Levi in the Gospels of Mark and Luke) was a Jew who was working for the Romans as a tax collector prior to being called by Jesus. The Gospels tell us that he was called by Jesus while sitting in the custom's house in Capernaum. It is believed that he preached among the Jews for fifteen years, but the details of his later life are uncertain. Some accounts point to him evangelizing in Ethiopia, others in Parthia or Persia. Matthew's Gospel is the first gospel of the New Testament. St. Matthew likely died a martyr's death possibly in the area of Egypt.

As Jesus passed on from there, he saw a man named Matthew sitting at the customs post. He said to him, "Follow me." And he got up and followed him. While he was at table in his house, many tax collectors and sinners came and sat with Jesus and his disciples. The Pharisees saw this and said to his disciples, "Why does your teacher eat with tax collectors and sinners?" He heard this and said, "Those who are well do not need a physician, but the sick do. Go and learn the meaning of the words, 'I desire mercy, not sacrifice.' I did not come to call the righteous but sinners."

—Matthew 9:9–13

SEPTEMBER 22

SAINT THOMAS OF VILLANOVA

(1488–1555) Bishop. Born in Castile, Spain, St. Thomas was educated in the town of Villanova. His parents taught him at an early age the value of charity to the poor, and it was a virtue he practiced diligently for his entire life. After years of study, he became a professor of philosophy. In 1518 he became an Augustinian and was ordained a priest in 1520. So driven to evangelize, he was known as the "Apostle of Spain." He was made Archbishop in 1544 but continued to live a life of great austerity and charity. This "father of the poor" worked unceasingly to help better the lives of the poor by establishing boarding schools, high schools, homeless shelters, and soup kitchens, as well as arranging for dowries for girls who could not afford them. St. Thomas was canonized in 1658 by Pope Alexander VII.

Rejoice, then, you poor people; shout for joy, you needy ones; because even if the world holds you in contempt you are highly valued by your Lord God and the angels.

—St. Thomas of Villanova

. . . .

SAINT PIO OF PIETRELCINA

(1887–1968) Priest. Born in Pietrelcina, Italy, Francecso Forgione joined the Capuchin Franciscans at the age of fifteen and adopted the name of Pio. He was ordained as a priest in 1910 and served a short time in the Italian army during World War I. In 1910, he first experienced the invisible Stigmata (the five wounds of the crucified Christ). He was sent on an assignment to the convent at San Giovanni Rotondo in 1916 and stayed there for the rest of his life. In 1918, the Stigmata became visible—on his hands, his feet, and his side. In 1956, he established a hospital called the Home for the Relief of Suffering, which was a long held dream of his. The only Catholic priest in the history of the Church to bear the stigmata, Padre Pio was canonized on June 16, 2002 by Pope John Paul II.

It is difficult to become a saint. Difficult, but not impossible. The road to perfection is long, as long as one's lifetime. Along the way, consolation becomes rest; but as soon as your strength is restored, you must diligently get up and resume the trip.

—St. Pio of Pietrelcina

At all times, try to conform to the will of God in everything that you do, and have no fear. This conformity is the surest way to Heaven.

—*St. Pio of Pietrelcina*

SAINT PACIFIC OF SAN SEVERINO

(1653–1721) Priest. Born in San Severino, Italy, St. Pacific lost his parents when he was three years old. He was raised by a strict uncle but offered up any hardships he endured to God. At the age of seventeen, he joined the Franciscans and was ordained at the age of twenty-five. He was assigned to minister to the people in the mountain villages of the Apennines and he was content to teach and spread the Gospels to the poor and uneducated people of the region. When he was almost forty, he was struck with a mysterious illness that left him deaf, blind, and disabled; he lived as a near invalid for thirty years. Rather than turning from God in despair, he redoubled his efforts at prayer and cultivated a saintly patience and humility that carried him through three decades of pain and suffering. St. Pacific was canonized by Pope Gregory XVI in 1839.

Blessed St. Pacific of San Severino, you who bore many years of suffering with humility and patience, offering your pain for the salvation of souls and the conversion of sinners, intercede for me on my behalf that I may shoulder my burdens with patience, strength, and humility. I ask this in Jesus' name. Amen.

SAINT CLEOPAS

(first century) Disciple. St. Cleopas was one of the disciples who met the Resurrected Jesus en route to Emmaus. The companion of St. Cleophas is unnamed in the Gospel.

That very day, the first day of the week, two of Jesus' disciples were going to a village seven miles from Jerusalem called Emmaus. . . . One of them, named Cleopas.

—Luke 24:13–25

. . . .

SAINT THERESA COUDERC

(b. 1805) Founder. Born to a wealthy family in France, St. Theresa attended a mission as a young woman and felt drawn to the religious life. With the guidance of a local priest, Father Terme, she joined the Daughters of St. Regis, whose aim was to serve the children in the villages where there was no Christian school. The order later evolved into the Cenacle Sisters, and St. Theresa and Father Terme worked together to establish a hostel for women pilgrims that later evolved into a spiritual retreat house for women. For the last ten years of her life St. Theresa suffered greatly in body and soul but maintained her strong faith and total surrender to God. She was canonized in 1970 by Pope Paul VI.

Lord Jesus, I unite myself to your perpetual, unceasing, universal sacrifice. I offer myself to you every day of my life and every moment of every day, according to your most holy and most lovable will. You have been the victim of my salvation, I wish to be the victim of your love. Accept my desire, take my offering, graciously hear my prayer: let me live by love, let me die of love, and let my last heartbeat be an act of the most perfect love.

—Prayer of St. Therese of Couderc

SAINT VINCENT DE PAUL

(c. 1581–1660) Born into a peasant family in Gascony, France, St. Vincent began his studies at a Franciscan college at the age of fourteen and was ordained at the age of nineteen. Some sources indicate that St. Vincent was kidnapped by pirates and held as a slave for two years until he was able to escape back to France. Once back in France, he became a tutor to the children of a wealthy family and started preaching missions. In 1625 he founded the Congregation of the Priests of the Mission or the Vincentians. His priests took the vows of poverty, chastity, obedience, and stability, and were committed to helping the poor and oppressed and alleviating suffering wherever it existed. St. Vincent also co-founded the Sisters of Charity together with St. Louise de Marillac. Known as the Apostle of Charity, St. Vincent died at the age of eighty and was canonized in 1737 by Pope Clement XII.

We cannot better assure our eternal happiness than by living and dying in the service of the poor, in the arms of Providence, and with genuine renouncement of ourselves in order to follow Jesus Christ.

—*St. Vincent de Paul*

Extend your mercy towards others, so that there can be no one in need whom you meet without helping. For what hope is there for us if God should withdraw His Mercy from us?

—*St. Vincent de Paul*

SAINT WENCESLAUS

(died 929) Martyr. Son of the duke of Bohemia, Saint Wenceslaus was taught Christianity by his grandmother, St. Ludmila. At the age of eighteen, he succeeded his father to the throne. He worked to convert his country to Christianity, built many churches, and fought for the freedom to worship against the pagan noblemen and his own brother who was pagan. Though he only reigned for a period of seven years, he was known for his charity and for being a wise and "Good King." One day, his jealous brother and his cronies attacked the saint as he was on his way to Mass. As he lay dying, he asked forgiveness for his brother.

This is the lesson we can learn from Saint Wenceslaus, who had the courage to prefer the kingdom of heaven to the enticement of worldly power. His gaze never moved away from Jesus Christ. . . . As an obedient disciple of the Lord, the young prince Wenceslaus remained faithful to the Gospel teachings he had learned from his saintly grandmother, the martyr Ludmila. In observing these, even before committing himself to build peaceful relations within his lands and with neighboring countries, he took steps to spread the Christian faith, summoning priests and building churches.

—Pope Benedict XVI, *from his homily on Feast of St. Wenceslaus,
Prague, September 28, 2009*

. . . .
SEPTEMBER 29

SAINTS MICHAEL, GABRIEL, AND RAPHAEL, ACHANGELS

This feast celebrates the three Archangels who are honored as both angels and saints. Of all of the angels in the Bible, these are the only three that are named.

Michael is said to be the most powerful of the Archangels. In the Old Testament he spoke to Abraham and appeared to Moses. The Torah describes Michael as the "great prince" who will protect God's people even during the struggle between good and evil at the end of the world. In Christianity, he is known as "the protector of all people." Michael the Archangel has been invoked as both patron and protector of Christians from the earliest days of the Church.

Gabriel has served as an important messenger for God. He appears in the Old Testament in several books; in the New Testament he appeared to Zechariah to announce the birth of St. John the Baptist, but the most important message Gabriel brought from God was the Annunciation. It was at the Annunciation that Gabriel revealed to Mary that she would bear a Son Who would be conceived of the Holy Spirit, Son of the Most High, and the Savior of the World. (Luke 1:26).

Rapheal first appears in the Torah in the Book of Tobit. Taking on human form, he guides young Tobiah on a journey to collect a debt owed to his father. After battling with the devil, then helping Tobiah find a wife, collecting the debt that is owed, and healing Tobit from his blindness, he reveals his true identity saying, "I am the Angel Rapheal, one of the seven who stand before the throne of God."

I call upon the angels and saints, who fly like eagles straight toward their fiery goal; their protection will defend me against the birds of prey that threaten to devour me. The spirits of evil cannot claim me for their own; I belong only to You, Jesus, You who have Your nest up there in the sun of love.

—St. Thérèse de Lisieux

SAINT JEROME

(c. 347–420) Priest and Doctor of the Church. Baptized in 366, St. Jerome sought out the religious life as a monk for many years and hermit. Dogmatic and prickly, he was famous for writing the Latin translation of the Bible called the Vulgate at the request of Pope Damasus. One of the greatest scholars of the early Church, he spent his last years in Bethlehem where he and other early saints founded monasteries and schools and where he died at almost eighty years of age.

No one loves to tell of scandal except to him who loves to hear it. Learn, then, to rebuke and check the detracting tongue by showing that you do not listen to it with pleasure.

—St. Jerome

OCTOBER

SAINT THÉRÈSE OF LISIEUX

(1873–1897) Religious and Doctor of the Church. Born in France as Marie Frances Thérèse Martin, she entered the Carmelite convent in Lisieux, Normandy when she was fifteen. At the request of her older sister Pauline (Mother Agnes), who was the prioress there, St. Thérèse wrote an autobiography that recounted her spiritual development called *The Story of A Soul*. In it, she describes her path to God which came to be known as "the little way." Believing that great deeds were not available to her, she was determined to humbly undertake whatever small deeds and sacrifices she could for the love of God. She died at twenty-four years old from tuberculosis. Published after her death, her autobiography was a great success. She was canonized in 1925 and made a Doctor of the Church by Pope John Paul II in 1997. St. Therese is the copatron of the missions with St. Francis Xavier and is one of the copatrons of France.

After my death, I will let fall a shower of roses. I will spend my heaven doing good upon earth. I will raise up a mighty host of little saints. My mission is to make God loved.

—St. Thérèse Lisieux

I say very simply to God what I wish to say, without composing beautiful sentences, and He always understands me.

—St. Thérèse Lisieux

Take O Lord, from our hearts all jealousy, indignation, wrath, and contention, and whatsoever may hurt charity and lesson brotherly love.

—St. Thérèse Lisieux

OPPOSITE: Saint Thérèse of Lisieux

THE GUARDIAN ANGELS

The belief that we each have a guardian angel assigned to protect and guide us through life dates back for centuries and is rooted in the Gospels. In 1615, the feast honoring the Guardian Angels was officially added to the Church calendar by Pope Paul V. While the feast was originally celebrated on September 29, it was moved to October 2 by Pope Clement X in 1670.

See that you do not despise one of these little ones, for I say to you that their angels in heaven always look upon the face of my heavenly Father.

—Matthew 18:10

So valuable to heaven is the dignity of the human soul that every member of the human race has a guardian angel from the moment the person begins to be.

—St. Jerome

Our Guardian Angels are our most faithful friends, because they are with us day and night, always and everywhere. We ought often to invoke them.

—St. John Vianney

Our turning aside from the way is not a loss to us only, but a weariness for the angels and for all the saints in Christ Jesus. Our humiliation gives grief to them all, and our salvation gives joy and refreshment to them all.

—St. Anthony of Egypt

When tempted, invoke your angel. Ignore the devil and do not be afraid of him: he trembles and flees at your guardian angel's sight.

—St. John Bosco

Angel of God, my guardian dear,
to whom God's love commits me here,

ever this day be at my side,
to light and guard, to rule and guide.
Amen.

—*Guardian Angel Prayer*

. . . .

SAINT MOTHER THEODORE GUERIN

(1798–1856) Religious, founder. Born in France as Anne-Therese, she was distraught at the murder of her father when she was a teenager. After caring for her mother and younger sister, she joined the Sisters of Providence and took the name of Sister St. Theodore. Though she was left enfeebled from an illness, she was an excellent teacher for seventeen years. In 1840, she and several of her sisters were sent to Indiana to care for the sick and impoverished and to help educate the children of pioneers. It was there that St. Mother Theodore began the arduous work of establishing the Sisters of Providence of Saint Mary-of-the-Woods. Facing many trials, obstacles, and setbacks, she finally prevailed in establishing the motherhouse and novitiate, as well as setting up schools, orphanages, and even free pharmacies. This courageous and determined saint was beatified in 1998 and canonized by Pope Benedict XVI in 2006.

The life of Blessed Theodora Guerin is a testimony that everything is possible with and for God.

—*Pope John Paul II, from the beatification Mass of Blessed Theodore Guerin*

. . . .

SAINT FRANCIS OF ASSISI

(1182–1226) Founder. Born to a wealthy family in Assisi, Italy, Francis was amiable but frivolous in his youth but was eventually led to a dramatic conversion. Taken as a prisoner in the war between Assisi and Perugia, Francis spent a year imprisoned in a dark dungeon and experienced deprivation for the first time in his life. He found solace in reaching out to his fellow prisoners and started to feel a yearning within his soul. In 1206, he was in Church kneeling in prayer when he heard the voice of God imploring him to "repair" the Church. Accepting God's challenge, Francis immediately sold his possessions and took to hiding in a cave for fear of his father. In a dramatic public trial, Francis stripped off his clothes and laid them at his father's feet and proclaimed that from hence forward he would only acknowledge his Father in heaven. He set out in the coarsest of clothes, begging for food, and preaching the Word of God, and soon found his first followers. In 1220, Francis and his disciples were granted permission by Pope Innocent III to form the Order of Friars Minor. Within a few short years the order had grown to more than five thousand. Two years prior to his death, St. Francis received the stigmata. Gravely ill and nearly blind, St. Francis died peacefully, surrounded by his brothers and whispering his prayers. He was forty-five years old. St. Francis was canonized less than two years later by Pope Gregory IX who broke down in tears during his homily about the great saint. Beloved and revered the world over, St. Francis is the patron of animals and the environment.

Most high, glorious God, enlighten the darkness of my heart and give me, Lord, a correct faith, a certain hope, a perfect charity, sense, and knowledge, so that I may carry out Your holy and true command.

—*St. Francis of Assisi*

Lord, make me an instrument of Your peace.
Where there is hatred, let me sow love;
Where there is injury, pardon;
Where there is friction, union;
Where there is error, truth;
Where there is doubt, faith;
Where there is despair, hope;
Where there is darkness, light;
Where there is sadness, joy.
O Divine Master, Grant that I may not so much seek

OPPOSITE: Saint Francis of Assisi

to be consoled as to console,
to be understood as to understand,
to be loved as to love.
For it is in giving that we receive.
It is in pardoning that we are pardoned.
It is in dying that we are born to eternal life.

—The Prayer of St. Francis, said throughout the world in his name.
It is believed to have been written in France in or about 1912.

Sanctify yourself and you will sanctify society.

—St. Francis of Assisi

I have been all things unholy. If God can work through me, He can work through anyone.

—St. Francis of Assisi

....

OCTOBER 5

SAINT MARIA FAUSTINA KOWALSKA

(1905–1938) Religious. Born as Helena, she was the third of ten children in a poor but devout farming family in Poland. Her formal education consisted of three years of school. As a teenager she left home and worked as a servant to help support herself and her family. In 1925, she joined the Congregation of the Sisters of Our Lady of Mercy, taking the name of Maria Faustina, and worked as a porter, in the kitchen, and in the garden of the convent. Possessed of a deep and mystical inner prayer life, she received many revelations from Jesus that she recorded in her now famous work, *The Diary of St. Maria Faustina Kowalska*. What was revealed to St. Maria Faustina by Jesus was His infinite mercy and compassion to all humankind. St. Faustina died of tuberculosis on October 5, 1938. She was beatified by Pope John Paul II in 1993 and canonized by him on April 30, 2000. At her canonization, Pope John Paul II deemed the second Sunday of Easter to be forever more celebrated as Divine Mercy Sunday throughout the Church.

In the Old Covenant I sent prophets wielding thunderbolts to My people. Today I am sending you with My mercy to the people of the whole world. I do not want to punish aching mankind, but I desire to heal it, pressing it to My Merciful Heart. I use punishment when they themselves force Me to do so; My hand is reluctant to take hold of the sword of justice. Before the Day of Justice I am sending the Day of Mercy.

—A revelation of Jesus to St. Maria Faustina, as recorded in her Diary

O my Jesus, each of Your saints reflects one of Your virtues; I desire to reflect Your compassionate heart, full of mercy; I want to glorify it. Let Your mercy, O Jesus, be impressed upon my heart and soul like a seal, and this will be my badge in this and the future life.

—St. Maria Faustina, from her Diary

Sister Faustina's canonization has a particular eloquence: by this act I intend today to pass this message on to the new millennium. I pass it on to all people, so that they will learn to know ever better the true face of God and the true face of their brethren.

—Pope John Paul II, from his homily at the canonization of St. Maria Faustina, April 2000

OCTOBER 6

BLESSED MARIE ROSE DUROCHER

(c. 1811–1849) Founder. Born into a large family in Quebec, Canada, Eulalie Durocher was schooled by the Sisters of Notre Dame. Desiring to join a religious community but plagued by poor health, she spent thirteen years working in a rectory doing the housework and organizing the pastoral activities. At the prodding of the bishop and of her spiritual director, she founded a new order known as the Sisters of the Holy Names of Jesus and Mary that was dedicated to the religious education of young girls. In spite of many obstacles and trials, she faithfully led her community until her death at the age of thirty-eight. Pope John Paul II declared her Blessed in 1982.

Since we tread along the same way, let us lend a hand to one another to help surmount the difficulties that present themselves.

—Blessed Marie Rose Durocher

OUR LADY OF THE ROSARY

This feast was originally celebrated under the name of the Feast of Our Lady of Victory, in recognition of the Christian victory against the Turks at the battle of Lepanto in 1571. In 1573, Pope Gregory XIII changed the name of the feast to the Feast of the Holy Rosary. In 1716, it was extended to the universal Church by Pope Clement XI and celebrated on the first Sunday of October. In 1913, Pope Pius X changed the date of the feast to October 7th. And in 1960, Pope John XXIII changed the name of the celebration to the Feast to Our Lady of the Holy Rosary. Though tradition holds that the Holy Rosary was revealed to St. Dominic by the Blessed Mother, it may have actually been begun by one of his followers, Blessed Alan de la Roche, who is known as the "apostle of the rosary," and is the founder of Confraternity of the Rosary in the fifteenth century.

The rosary, though clearly Marian in character, is at heart a Christ-centered prayer. It has all the depth of the gospel message in its entirety.

—Pope John Paul II

The Most Holy Virgin in these last times in which we live has given a new efficacy to the recitation of the Rosary to such an extent that there is no problem, no matter how difficult it is, whether temporal or above all spiritual, in the personal life of each one of us, of our families…that cannot be solved by the Rosary. There is no problem, I tell you, no matter how difficult it is, that we cannot resolve by the prayer of the Holy Rosary.

—Sister Lucia dos Santos, to whom the
Blessed Mother appeared at Fatima

The Rosary is the most beautiful and the most rich in graces of all prayers; it is the prayer that touches most the Heart of the Mother of God. . . . And if you wish peace to reign in your homes, recite the family Rosary.

—*St. Pius X*

The Rosary is my favorite prayer. A marvelous prayer! Marvelous in its simplicity and in its depth.

—*Pope John Paul II*

OCTOBER 8

SAINT PELAGIA

(died c. 311) Virgin, martyr. St. Pelagia was a young Christian woman who was targeted for her faith during the Christian persecutions under Emperor Diocletian. It is believed that when the soldiers came to arrest her, she threw herself from the rooftop of her house to preserve her virginity. The story of her martyrdom was spoken of and praised by St. Ambrose and St. John Chrysostom.

I saw myself dying with a desire to see God, and I knew not how to seek that life other than by dying. Over my spirit flash and float in divine radiancy the bright and glorious visions of the world to which I go.

—*St. Teresa of Avila*

OCTOBER 9

SAINT JOHN LEONARDI

(c. 1541–1609) Priest. Born in Lucca, Italy, St. John was drawn to a religious life even as a child. He was ordained at the age of thirty-two and devoted himself to helping those in need especially the sick and imprisoned. In 1583 he laid the foundations for what would become the Clerks Regular of the Mother of

God. A great defender of the faith, he is one of the founders of the College for the Propagation of the Faith. Continually devoting himself to those in need, he succumbed to illness after ministering to victims of the plague. St. John died in 1609 and was canonized by Pope Pius XI in 1938.

Do not be afraid any longer, little flock, for your Father is pleased to give you the kingdom. Sell your belongings and give alms. Provide money bags for yourselves that do not wear out, an inexhaustible treasure in heaven that no thief can reach nor moth destroy.

—*St. John Leonardi*

. . . .

OCTOBER 10

SAINT FRANCIS BORGIA

(1510–1572) Priest. St. Francis was born in Spain, a member of the legendary Borgia family. Francis was an upright duke of Granada. After he was widowed, he felt drawn to a religious life and joined the Jesuits. A passionate preacher, he founded monasteries all through Spain and Portugal. In 1561, he was named the Governor General of the Jesuits and he went on to organize the first missions to the New World. Called the "second founder" of the Jesuits, St. Francis Borgia was canonized in 1671.

We must perform all our works in God and refer them to His glory so that they will be permanent and stable. Everyone—whether kings, nobles, tradesmen or peasants—must do all things for the glory of God and under the inspiration of Christ's example.

—*St. Francis Borgia*

SAINT JOHN XXIII

(1881–1963) Pope. Angelo Giuseppe Roncalli was the first son born to a northern Italian farming family. Proud of his humble roots, he entered the seminary at Bergamo in 1892 and was ordained a priest in 1904. He went to Rome to continue his studies and served as the secretary to the bishop of Bergamo, taught in a seminary, acted as the publisher of a diocesan newspaper, and served as a stretcher-bearer during World War I. In 1925, he became a papal diplomat in Bulgaria, Turkey, and France. During World War II, he helped many Jews escape Nazi persecution by issuing "transit visas" and tried to implement rescue efforts with other ambassadors. Rising through the liturgical ranks, he was named an archbishop, cardinal, and patriarch of Venice, then elected pope in 1958 when he was nearly seventy-eight years old. Taking the name of John, he was known as a humble, down to earth, and dynamic pope who was involved in the world peace process and in promoting social justice. He is perhaps best known for the Second Vatican Council, which initiated major reforms in the Church, as well as with other Christian sects and other religions. Pope John XXIII died from cancer in June of 1963. He was beatified by Pope John Paul II in 2000 and canonized together with Pope John Paul II by Pope Francis on April 27, 2014, Divine Mercy Sunday.

To have accepted with simplicity the honour and the burden of the pontificate, with the joy of being able to say that I did nothing to obtain it, absolutely nothing; indeed I was most careful and conscientious to avoid anything that might direct attention to myself. As the voting in Conclave wavered to and fro, I rejoiced when I saw the chances of my being elected diminishing and the likelihood of others, in my opinion truly most worthy and venerable persons, being chosen.

—St. John XXIII, *from his autobiography,* Journal of A Soul

The Ecumenical Council will surely be, even more than a new and magnificent Pentecost, a real and new Epiphany, one of the many revelations which have been renewed and are continually being renewed in the course of history, but one of the greatest of all.

—St. John XXIII, *on the Second Vatican Council*

Consult not your fears but your hopes and your dreams. Think not about your frustrations, but about your unfulfilled potential. Concern yourself not with what you tried and failed in, but with what it is still possible for you to do.

—*St. John XXIII*

. . . .

OCTOBER 12

SAINT WILFRID

(634–709) Bishop. Born to a noble family in Northumberland, he entered the famous monastery of Lindisfarne in 648, and set out for Rome and Lyons for several years. Returning to Northumberland, he was made abbot at the newly formed monastery at Ripon. In 664, he was instrumental at the Synod of Whitby where it was decided to refer to the Roman calendar rather than the Celtic calendar for calculating the date of Easter. Appointed Bishop of York, he built many churches, founded monasteries, and introduced the Benedictine Rule to the region. He was also embroiled in a number of controversies which resulted in him being exiled twice from his diocese and over which he repeatedly sought intervention from Rome. In 703, he resigned his position and spent his last years at his monastery at Ripon where he was again able to focus on prayer and penance.

O Blessed St. Wilfrid, you who faithfully led your flock and bore trials and tribulations with patience, help me to bear the challenges and trials of my life with fortitude and grace. I ask this in the name of Jesus Christ, our Lord and Savior. Amen.

. . . .

OCTOBER 13

SAINT GERALD OF AURILLAC

(855–909) Founder. Born to a noble family in France, St. Gerald inherited his father's title as Count of Auvergne, but chose to give away the bulk of his wealth and property to those in need. He chose a simple, prayerful life, maintaining a vow of chastity, while carrying out his duties as a nobleman. Later, after completing a pilgrimage to Rome, St. Gerald founded a Benedictine monastery at Aurillac. Desiring to join the Benedictines himself, he was dissuaded from doing so by St. Gausbert who persuaded him that his true vocation was to serve God as a lay person. Suffering from blindness at the end of his life, St. Gerald died in 909. He is the patron saint of bachelors, counts, and the Upper Auvergne region of France.

O Blessed St. Gerald, you lived your life as a faithful follower of Christ while carrying out your worldly duties and responsibilities, help me to discern my true vocation from God and give me the strength to follow God's path for me to the best of my abilities. I ask this in the name of Jesus Christ. Amen.

SAINT CALLISTUS I

(died c. 223) Pope and martyr. A Christian slave in a noble Roman family, the future saint fled after losing money belonging to his master. Sentenced to a period of hard labor, he was later freed by some fellow Christians, and called by the pope to oversee the Christian cemetery near the Catacombs. After serving as a deacon he was elected pope in 217. His papacy was vehemently opposed by the future St. Hippolytus who set himself up as the first antipope and ushered in a schism in the Church that lasted close to twenty years. St. Hippolytus, a martyr himself, eventually reconciled with Rome and urged his followers to reunite with the Church. St. Callistus died as a martyr in the Christian persecutions of 222. He is the first pope after St. Peter to be venerated as a martyr in the Church.

Christ, like a skillful physician, understands the weakness of men. He loves to teach the ignorant and the erring He turns again to His own true way. He is easily found by those who live by faith and to those of pure eye and holy heart, who desire to knock at the door, He opens immediately.

—St. Hippolytus of Rome

SAINT TERESA OF AVILA

(1515–1582) Founder and Doctor of the Church. Born in Avila, Spain, and educated by Augustinian nuns, St. Teresa was a spirited and intelligent girl who heard God's call as a young woman. Determined to enter the religious life, she joined the Carmelite Convent of the Incarnation in Avila in 1534. Dissatisfied with the state of her order, she undertook the herculean task of reforming it and restoring it to its primitive Rule. With the guidance of St. John of the Cross, St. Teresa established the Reform of the Discalced Carmelites for both the sisters and brothers of her order. A mystic who was graced with many spiritual gifts including ecstasies and levitation, St. Teresa's writings establish her as a towering figure among Christian thinkers. Bold, contemplative, and complex, St. Teresa of Avila was canonized in 1622 by Pope Gregory XV. She was declared a Doctor of the Church by Pope Paul VII in 1970 together with St. Catherine of Siena. They are the first women honored as Doctors of the Church.

I would willingly endure all the sufferings of this world to be raised a degree higher in Heaven, and to possess the smallest increase of the knowledge of God's greatness.

—*St. Teresa of Avila*

There is more value in a little study of humility and in a single act of it than in all the knowledge in the world.

—*St. Teresa of Avila*

No wonder you have so few friends, since this is the way you treat them.
—*St. Teresa was heard praying this to God after a cart she was riding in en route to founding another Carmelite convent overturned.*

Be kind to all and severe to thyself.

—*St. Teresa of Avila*

OPPOSITE: Saint Teresa of Avila

SAINT GERARD OF MAJELLA

(1726–1755) Religious. Born in Italy to a humble family, St. Gerard joined the Redemptorists when he was twenty-three. Filled with simple wisdom and a great humility, St. Gerard possessed many extraordinary spiritual gifts such as reading souls, bilocation, and miraculous healings. Dying at the age of twenty-nine from tuberculosis, St. Gerard was canonized in 1904 by St. Pius X. He is the patron of expectant mothers and of women desiring motherhood.

Be courageous, do not be cast down. Trust in God and hope that He will grant you every grace. Do not rely on yourself, but rather on the Lord, and if you imagine that all is calm, then be assured that the enemy is quite near. Do not put too much confidence in peace, for in the midst of rest war may break out.

—*St. Gerard of Majella*

O good St. Gerard, powerful intercessor before God and wonder worker of our day, confidently I call upon you and seek your aid. On Earth you always fulfilled God's designs, help me now to do the holy will of God. Implore the Master of Life, from whom all paternity proceeds, to render me fruitful in offspring, that I may raise up children to God in this life, and in the world to come, heirs to the Kingdom of His Glory. Amen.

—*Prayer to St. Gerard for Motherhood*

ST. IGNATIUS OF ANTIOCH

(died c. 107) Bishop, martyr. Born in Antioch, St. Ignatius likely converted to Christianity as an adult and was a disciple of St. John the Evangelist. He was appointed the bishop of Antioch by St. Peter. Seeking a martyr's death, St. Ignatius was arrested and condemned to die for his faith during Emperor

Trajan's reign. En route from Antioch to Rome, St. Ignatius wrote seven letters imploring Christians to remain steadfast in their faith. Once in Rome, St. Ignatius was brought to the Colosseum and torn apart by lions.

I am God's wheat and shall be ground by the teeth of wild animals. I am writing to all the churches to let it be known that I will gladly die for God if only you do not stand in my way. I plead with you: show me no untimely kindness. Let me be food for the wild beasts, for they are my way to God. I am God's wheat and shall be ground by their teeth so that I may become Christ's pure bread. Pray to Christ for me that the animals will be the means of making me a sacrificial victim for God. No earthly pleasures, no kingdoms of this world can benefit me in any way. I prefer death in Christ Jesus to power over the farthest limits of the earth. He who died in place of us is the one object of my quest. He who rose for our sakes is my one desire.

—*St. Ignatius of Antioch, Letter to the Romans*

. . . .

OCTOBER 18

SAINT LUKE

(first century) Apostle. A native of Antioch, St. Luke was a Greek physician before converting to Christianity. Among St. Paul's first disciples, St. Luke was a dear and faithful friend to St. Paul with whom he made many missionary journeys. St. Luke is believed to be the writer of the Gospel According to Luke as well as the Acts of the Apostles. Written for a Gentile Christian audience, St. Luke's Gospel focuses on Jesus as the Savior of mankind and on his compassion and mercy. It is believed St. Luke was crucified in his old age with St. Andrew.

Almighty God, who inspired Your servant Luke the Physician to set forth in the Gospel the love and healing power of Your Son: Graciously continue in Your Church the love and power to heal, to the praise and glory of Your Name, through Jesus Christ, our Lord. Amen.

—*Prayer Honoring St. Luke*

SAINT PETER OF ALCÁNTARA

(1499–1562) Religious, founder. Born in Alcántara, Spain, St. Peter heard God's call while he was studying at the University of Salamanca and joined the Franciscans. Observing the rule with uncompromising strictness, he later founded a reform branch of the Franciscans called the Alcantarines. Known for his legendary patience and passionate preaching, he was the spiritual director, confessor, and friend to St. Teresa of Avila, St. Peter was canonized in 1669.

Our Lord in the Blessed Sacrament has His hands full of graces, and He is ready to bestow them on anyone who asks for them.

—*St. Peter of Alcántara*

Truly, matters in the world are in a bad state; but if you and I begin in earnest to reform ourselves, a really good beginning will have been made.

—*St. Peter of Alcántara*

SAINT PAUL OF THE CROSS

(1694–1775) Priest, founder. Born to poor but noble parents in Italy, St. Paul had a series of visions impelling him to start a new religious order. After prayerful consideration and with the counsel of his bishop, St. Paul and his brother John were ordained priests and later co-founded the Order of the Passionists. Devoted to preaching about the Passion of Christ, St. Paul was a fiery preacher who was responsible for the conversion of many who heard his impassioned sermons. St. Paul of the Cross was canonized in 1867 by Pope Pius IX.

I hope that God will save me through the merits of the Passion of Jesus. The more difficulties in life, the more I hope in God. By God's grace I will not lose my soul, but I hope in His mercy.

—St. Paul of the Cross

. . . .

OCTOBER 21

BLESSED JOSEPHINE LEROUX

(1747–1794) Religious, martyr. Born Ann-Joseph Leroux in Cambral, France, she entered the Poor Clares when she was twenty-two. She fled back to her family when her community was forced to disband during the Reign of Terror of the French Revolution. She returned to religious life in 1793 when she and her sister, Marie Scholastique, an Ursuline nun, went to the Ursuline convent. The Revolutionaries came to arrest them in 1794 and within days they were convicted of high treason for their faith and sentenced to die. Blessed Josephine, Sister Marie, and several other nuns were executed by the guillotine. Blessed Josephine was said to kiss the hand of her executioner and extend her forgiveness to her persecutors before her death.

Dear brothers and sisters . . . we are probably not called to martyrdom, but not one of us is excluded from the divine call to holiness, to attain the high standard of Christian living, and this entails taking up our daily cross. All of us, especially in our time when selfishness and individualism seem to prevail, must take on as a first and fundamental commitment the duty to grow every day in greater love for God and for our brothers and sisters, to transform our own lives and thereby transform the life of our world too. Through the intercession of the Saints and Martyrs let us ask the Lord to set our hearts on fire so that we may be able to love as he has loved each one of us.

—Pope Benedict, XVI, 2010

SAINT JOHN PAUL II

(1920–2005) Pope. Born in Wadowice, Poland as Karol Wojtyla, he faced many losses in his early life. His mother died when he was nine and his older brother died three years later. Before his twenty-first birthday, his beloved father died as well. Amid all of the devastating loss he had suffered, he heard God calling him to serve. He was ordained a priest in 1946, and headed to Rome where he earned two doctorate degrees. Returning to Poland, he taught philosophy and ethics to packed lecture halls at Catholic University of Lublin. At thirty-eight, he was named the youngest bishop in Poland; and he went on to become the Archbishop of Krakow and then cardinal in 1967. In 1978, he surprised the world with his election to the papacy. Pope John Paul II had the third longest pontificate in the history of the church and led the Catholics of the world for nearly twenty-seven years. All through his papacy he brought the message of Christ to the world; he traveled the globe and connected with millions of people. A tireless promoter of ecumenism, he worked to bring together Christians and non-Christians alike. Prolific in his papacy, he wrote fourteen encyclicals and five books; he canonized 482 saints and beatified 1,338 people. Suffering from Parkinson's disease for the last years of his life, he was forced to slow his schedule down. He died at the age of eighty-four and more than four million pilgrims traveled to Vatican City to pay homage to the great leader. He was beatified by Pope Benedict XVI on May 1, 2011. In 2013, Pope Francis signed the papal degree in recognition of the second miracle attributed to Blessed John Paul II, and Pope Francis canonized the saintly pope on April 27, 2014.

Do not abandon yourselves to despair. We are the Easter people and Alleluia is our song.

—*Pope John Paul II*

We can think of the Holy Spirit as the soul of our soul, and thus the secret of our sanctification. Let us dwell in His powerful and discreet, intimate and transforming presence!

—*Pope John Paul II*

OPPOSITE: Saint John Paul II

Whenever violence is done in the name of religion, we must make it clear to everyone that in such instances we are not dealing with true religion.

—*Pope John Paul II*

....

OCTOBER 23

SAINT JOHN OF CAPESTRANO

(1386–1456) Religious. Born in Capestrano, Italy, St. John had a burgeoning legal career when he was imprisoned on politically motivated charges. After his release, he felt drawn to the religious life, and joined the Friars Minor in 1415. He was an inspired preacher and later established the Franciscan Observant Friars. He preached throughout Europe, Russia, and the Holy Land. He died at the age of seventy, several months after leading seventy-thousand Christians to victory at the Seige of Belgrade during the Crusades. This fearless saint was canonized in 1690.

Those who are called to the table of the Lord must glow with the brightness that comes from the good example of a praiseworthy and blameless life. They must completely remove from their lives the filth and uncleanness of vice. Their upright lives must make them like the salt of the earth for themselves and for the rest of mankind. The brightness of their wisdom must make them like the light of the world that brings light to others.

—*St. John of Capestrano*

....

OCTOBER 24

SAINT ANTHONY MARY CLARET

(1807–1870) Priest, bishop. Born in Spain in 1807, he assisted his father in the weaving trade before discerning his call to the religious life. Ordained a priest in 1835, he strongly desired to do missionary work, but his frail health stood in the way. He did establish a missionary order: The Missionary Sons of the Immaculate Heart of Mary or the Claretians. Made archbishop of Santiago in Cuba, he instituted many reforms and founded the Teaching Sisters of Mary Immaculate. Returning to Spain, he became the confessor of Queen Isabella II and followed her into exile after the Spanish Revolution of 1868. A prolific writer, St. Anthony is said to have written more than one-hundred-forty books and preached twenty-five-thousand sermons. In addition to preaching and writing, he also established schools, a library, a museum, and a science lab. Known for his devotion to the Blessed Sacrament and the Immaculate Heart of Mary, this dynamic saint was canonized in 1950 by Pope Pius XII.

Mary is the heart of the Church. This is why all works of charity spring from her. It is well known that the heart has two movements: systole and diastole. Thus Mary is always performing these two movements: absorbing grace from her Most Holy Son, and pouring it forth on sinners.

—St. Anthony Mary Claret

OCTOBER 25

SAINT JOHN ROBERTS

(1577–1610) Priest, martyr. Born in Wales to a farming family, St. John studied at Oxford for two years and then began studying law. Baptized a Protestant, St. John traveled to Paris where he converted to Catholicism and went to Spain where he joined the Benedictine Order. Ordained a priest in 1602, he returned to England and ministered tirelessly to victims of the Plague of 1603. He was arrested and banished from England on several occasions, only to return and continue spreading the faith. He was arrested for the last time in 1610 as he was saying Mass. Taken into custody in his vestments, he was executed within days at Tyburn. He was thirty-three. St. John Roberts was canonized as one of the Forty Martyrs of England and Wales by Pope Paul VI in 1970.

Life is given us that we may learn to die well, and we never think of it! To die well we must live well.

—St. John Vianney

. . . .

OCTOBER 26

SAINT EVARISTUS

(died c. 112) Pope, martyr. Believed to be from a family of Greek and Jewish origins from Bethlehem or Antioch, St. Evaristus converted to Christianity and became the successor to St. Pope Clement. He led the Church for a period of about eight years during the reign of Trajan. He is said to have divided Rome into parishes, assigned a priest to each parish, and named seven deacons to serve and assist the pope. Tradition points to him dying a martyr's death though it is not historically established.

Reckon up the priests from the days that Peter sat, and in their ancestral ranks note who succeeded whom; for that is the Rock over which the gates of hell shall never prevail.

—St. Augustine of Hippo

It is on Peter that He builds the Church, and to him that He entrusts the sheep to feed. And although He assigns a like power to all the Apostles, yet He founded a single chair, thus establishing by His own authority the source and hallmark of the Church's unity.

—St. Cyprian of Carthage

. . . .

OCTOBER 27

SAINT LUIGI GUANELLA

(1842–1915) Priest, founder. Born to a poor family in the Southern Alps of Italy, St. Luigi was ordained in 1866 and served as a parish priest. He later joined the Order of the Salesian priests, led by St. John Bosco. He founded several religious communities including the Daughters of St. Mary of Providence, the Pious Union of St. Joseph, and the Servants of Charity Congregation. His communities were devoted to caring for the elderly, disabled, homeless and abandoned children, and the sick and incurable. In 1912, St. Luigi sailed for America and began his work among the Italian immigrants of Chicago. In 1915, he returned to Italy after a deadly earthquake hit central Italy. He worked around the clock ministering to the thousands of people affected. Physically weakened from this trial, St. Luigi died later that year and is considered a martyr of charity. He was canonized in October of 2011 by Pope Benedict XVI.

O my Jesus, draw me entirely to you. Draw me with all the love of my heart. If I knew that one fiber of my heart did not palpitate for you, I would tear it out at any cost. But I know that I could not speak without your help. Draw me, O my Jesus, draw me completely. I know it well, my heart cannot rest until it rests in your heart.

—St. Luigi Guanella

. . . .

OCTOBER 28

SAINT JUDE AND SAINT SIMON

(first century) Apostles, martyrs. St. Jude (Thaddeus) was the brother of James the Less. According to the Gospel of John, St. Jude was at the Last Supper. Simon is also referenced in the Gospels in places as the "Zealot." It is unknown whether this refers to his life prior to his conversion or is a reference to his zealous evangelizing. After Pentecost, they set forth to evangelize. It is believed that they were both martyred in Persia. St. Jude is universally known as the patron of hopeless or lost causes. St. Simon is the patron of tanners and woodcutters.

O God, we thank you for the blessed Apostles, and especially for St. Simon and St. Jude. We pray that through their intercession we may be strengthened in our faith and zealous in our mission to serve You in this life and be joined together with You in Heaven. We ask this in the name of Jesus Christ, our Lord and Savior.

SAINT NARCISSUS OF JERUSALEM

(third century) Bishop. It is believed that St. Narcissus was the thirtieth bishop of Jerusalem and that he was nearly eighty when he was so named. Together with other bishops, he was instrumental at the Council which determined that Easter must always fall on a Sunday rather than coinciding with the Jewish Passover. The subject of false and defamatory accusations, he was ultimately exonerated but retreated into solitude and prayer for several years. He is said to have returned to his See in Jerusalem toward the end of his life.

In the midst of adversities, I desire prosperous days; in the midst of prosperity, I dread adversity. Between these two, is there no middle ground where the life of man is not a trial?

—*St. Augustine of Hippo*

SAINT ALPHONSUS RODRIGUEZ

(1533–1617) Religious. Born in Spain, St. Alphonsus helped his mother in the family wool business after the death of his father. He later married and had a son. By 1571, his wife had died during childbirth, his mother died, and his business was failing. He took his son to his sister's and began to focus on prayer and meditation. He desired to become a Jesuit but was denied due to his lack of education. He struggled through his studies and was finally accepted as a Jesuit brother in 1571. He became the doorkeeper at the Jesuit college in Majorca—a post he held for forty-five years. He had a great impact on many of the people coming and going there and served as a spiritual advisor for many of the students. Though he devoted himself to prayer and mortification, he was continually tempted and experienced periods of vast spiritual dryness. Battling disease, this gentle saint died in 1617 and was canonized in 1888.

As love is paid for in love, I must imitate Him, sharing in spirit all His sufferings. I must consider how much I owe Him and what He has done for me. Putting these sufferings between God and my soul, I must say, "What does it matter, my God, that I should endure for your love these small hardships? For you, Lord, endured so many great hardships for me.

—St. Alphonsus Rodriguez

OCTOBER 31

SAINT WOLFGANG

(c. 934– c. 994) Bishop. Born into a noble family in the German region of Swabia, St. Wolfgang was privately tutored as a child and later studied at the acclaimed Monastery of Reichenau. Discerning a religious vocation after teaching for a time, he joined the Benedictine monks in 964 and was ordained a priest in 968. Though he would have preferred a quiet, monastic life, he was sent on a missionary journey to evangelize the Magyars in 972. Later that year, he was named Bishop of Ratisbon (in today's Bavaria) though he retained his monastic habit and his ascetic lifestyle. A great reformer, he reformed the clergy in his diocese, rebuilt monasteries, built schools, and he was so focused on charity to the poor that he became known as "The Great Almoner." This dynamic yet contemplative bishop died in 994 and was canonized in 1052.

The poor had always the greatest share in his table and revenues, though in his profuse charities, he seemed to conceal from his own left hand what his right hand gave. The time which was not taken up in business, he consecrated entirely to the strictest silence and retirement; and he employed a considerable part of the nights in devout prayer. Not content with this, he sometimes retired into some remote cell for a time, and once lay a long time concealed in a wilderness, that by heavenly contemplation he might repair and nourish his own soul.

—The Lives of the Saints *by Rev. Alban Butler, about St. Wolfgang*

OPPOSITE: Saint Wolfgang

NOVEMBER

NOVEMBER 1

ALL SAINTS

The commemoration of "all the martyrs" was celebrated as early as the fourth century in the Eastern Church. In the West, the feast dates back to the seventh century when Pope Boniface IV converted the Pantheon of Rome to a Christian Church dedicated to the Blessed Virgin and all of the saints. In 835, Pope Gregory IV extended the feast honoring all of the saints to the universal Church and moved it to November 1. In the Eastern Church, the feast is celebrated on the first Sunday after Pentecost.

Those from whom I receive the greatest consolation and encouragement are those whom I know to be dwelling in Paradise.

—St. Teresa of Avila

This daring ambition of aspiring to great sanctity has never left me. I don't rely on my own merits, because I haven't any; I put all my confidence in Him who is virtue, who is holiness itself.

—Saint Thérèse of Lisieux

If they, why not I?—If these men and women could become saints, why cannot I with the help of Him who is all-powerful?

—St. Augustine of Hippo

ALL SOULS

The tradition of praying for the dead is practiced in Judaism and dates back to the earliest days of the Church. It is rooted in the belief that we on earth can help to shorten the journey of souls into heaven through our prayers and intercession. The commemoration of the feast on November 2 originated at the end of the tenth century when St. Odilo decreed that all monasteries of Cluny would honor the dead on that date. The practice spread to all Benedictine monasteries and was finally adopted by the Church in 1311. In 1915, Pope Benedict XV deemed that priests may celebrate three masses on All Souls' Day—for his own intentions, for the intentions of the pope, and for the faithful departed.

In your hands, O Lord,
we humbly entrust our brothers and sisters.
In this life you embraced them with your tender love;
deliver them now from every evil
and bid them eternal rest.
The old order has passed away:
welcome them into paradise,
where there will be no sorrow, no weeping or pain,
but fullness of peace and joy
with your Son and the Holy Spirit
forever and ever. Amen.

—Catholic Prayer for the Dead

NOVEMBER 3

SAINT MARTIN DE PORRES

(1579–1639) Lay Brother. Born in Lima, Peru, St. Martin was the illegitimate son of a Spanish knight, John de Porres, and a freed black slave from Panama, Anna Velasquez. His father didn't acknowledge his son for eight years and then left the family when a second child was born. At the age of twelve, St. Martin apprenticed with a barber-surgeon. At fifteen, he became a "lay helper" with the Dominicans in Lima, and after nine years he was asked by them to profess his vows. He spent the rest of his life there caring for the sick and poor, black and white alike. Though he desperately wanted to embark on a missionary journey and die a martyr's death, he never had the opportunity. He was instrumental in opening an orphanage for slaves from Africa and was in charge of the daily distribution of alms to those in need. Graced with a myriad of spiritual gifts, including bilocation and miraculous healing, he was immediately venerated as a saint upon his death. St. Martin was beatified in 1837, and was canonized by Pope John XXIII in 1962.

Compassion is preferable to cleanliness. Reflect that with a little soap I can easily clean my bed covers, but even with a torrent of tears I would never wash from my soul the stain that my harshness toward the unfortunate would create.

> —*St. Martin de Porres, to his brothers who rebuked him for allowing a sick beggar to rest in his own bed while he cared for the man.*

....

NOVEMBER 4

SAINT CHARLES BORROMEO

(1538–1584) Bishop, cardinal. Born in Arona, Italy, into a noble family, St. Charles was highly intelligent and received his doctorate degree in both civil and canon law. He was made a cardinal by his uncle, Pope Pius IV, who soon thereafter made Charles the archbishop of Milan at the young age of twenty-two. The future saint soon proved himself to be a brilliant reformer, innovator, and administrator. A key figure in organizing the Council of Trent, he also ministered heroically to the people of Milan during the great plague of 1575. Worn out by his life of service and severe penance, this dynamic saint died at the age of forty-six. St. Charles was canonized in 1610 by Pope Paul V and is the patron of seminarians.

. . . .

NOVEMBER 5

SAINT BERTILLE

(died 692) Religious. St. Bertille was born in the region of Soissons, France. As a young girl she gave her life to God and as soon as she was old enough she joined a monastery of nuns at Jouarre. Growing in virtue, wisdom, and confidence, she was given many diverse responsibilities such as caring for the children being educated at the monastery, ministering to the sick, and extending hospitality to visitors. She was eventually made the prioress and was of great assistance to the abbess. Later, she became an abbess herself at the restored monastery of Notre Dame de Chelles. There, she led her community with great vitality for more than forty-five years. St. Bertille was so well known for her holiness and the discipline of her monastery that she had two former queens join her community. A saint who combined wise leadership and great humility, St. Bertille died peacefully in her old age.

The holy abbess, who saw two great queens every day at her feet, seemed the most humble and the most fervent among her sisters, and showed by her conduct that no one commands well or with safety who has not first learned, and is not always ready, to obey well.
—*from* The Lives of the Saints *by Reverend Alban Butler, 1866, about St. Bertille*

SAINT LEONARD OF NOBLAC

(sixth century) Hermit, abbot. Born into the French nobility, St. Leonard was converted to Christianity by St. Remigius. Though he was offered the office of bishop, he turned it down to live instead as a hermit. It is said that King Clovis I and his pregnant wife were visiting the saint when the queen went into labor. St. Leonard was able to safely deliver the baby and in gratitude King Clovis granted him land for a monastery which became Noblac Abbey, later called Saint-Leonard. The king also vowed to free any prisoners whom the saint visited. Greatly venerated in the Middle Ages, St. Leonard is the patron for prisoners and women in labor.

O Blessed St. Leonard, you who ministered to prisoners during your lifetime, hear and bless our prayer for those men and women in prison today. Through your intercession, help them to find repentance and seek God's forgiveness. Give them and their families the gifts of hope and patience in their trials. We ask this through Christ our Lord. Amen.

SAINT WILLIBRORD

(c. 658–739) Priest, missionary. Born in Northumberland, St. Willibrord was educated at Ripon, England before traveling to Ireland at twenty years of age to study with St. Egbert. After years of study, he was ordained and embarked on a missionary journey to the north of Europe. He sought papal approval for his mission and was named archbishop to the Frisians. He succeeded in spreading the Gospel, building churches, and monasteries. He extended his missionary work to Denmark where he faced constant danger from enraged pagans. As new rulers came to power in the region, the saint saw much of his hard work undone, but he began again to spread the Good News, receiving a great deal of assistance from St. Boniface. St. Willibrord is known as an Apostle of Frisia and the Netherlands.

Let us work as if success depends on us alone, but with the heartfelt conviction that we are doing nothing and God everything.

—St. Ignatius Loyola

....

NOVEMBER 8

SAINT GODFREY

(c. 1066–1115) Bishop. Born to a noble family in France, he was sent at the age of five to live in the Benedictine Abbey where his godfather was the abbot. When he came of age, he took vows there himself and was ordained a priest. In 1096, he himself became abbot of a monastery in the diocese of Rheims which had fallen into utter disrepair. It was overrun with weeds and only a handful of brothers were in residence. Using every ounce of energy he had and with reliance on God, he worked to renovate, rebuild, and revitalize the monastery, and was able to bring it back to vitality. Deeming himself unworthy, he turned down the bishopric of Rheims but was later instructed to accept the office of bishop for Amiens. Known for his austerity, he was an enforcer of celibacy for the religious, and a vocal opponent of simony and drunkenness. In 1114, he returned to monastic life, but was ordered to return to Amiens as bishop. He died before he could do so.

A monastery is an academy of strict correction, where each one should allow himself to be treated, planed, and polished, so that, all the angles being effaced, he may be joined, united, and fastened to the will of God.

—St. Francis de Sales

BLESSED ELIZABETH OF THE TRINITY

(1880–1906) Religious. Elizabeth Catez was the first child born to a military family; she was born on her father's military base in France. Known as a willful child, she was famous for her passionate nature and for throwing tantrums. Her father died when she was young and her mother, her one sister, and Elizabeth moved very close to the Carmelite monastery in Dijon. A normal teen that enjoyed school, music, friends, and travel, Elizabeth also began to grow in her spirituality. She eventually discerned a spiritual vocation. At her mother's request, she waited until the age of twenty-one before she joined the Carmelites in Dijon and took the name of Elizabeth of the Trinity. She grew in virtue and wisdom as a Carmelite, devoting herself to reading the Gospels, hours of prayer, and serving her community. In 1905 she developed Addison's disease and spent eight months in the infirmary. She died at the age of twenty-six in 1906. Blessed Elizabeth was beatified in 1984 by Pope John Paul II.

It seems to me that I have found my heaven on earth, because my heaven is you, my God, and you are in my soul. You in me, and I in you—may this be my motto. What a joyous mystery is your presence within me, in that intimate sanctuary of my soul where I can always find you, even when I do not feel your presence. Of what importance is feeling? Perhaps you are all the closer when I feel you less.

—*Blessed Elizabeth of the Trinity*

The Trinity—this is our dwelling, our "home," the Father's house that we must never leave.

—*Blessed Elizabeth of the Trinity*

SAINT LEO THE GREAT

(d. 461) Pope and Doctor of the Church. Born in Tuscany, St. Leo was elected to the papacy in the year 440 and vigorously led the Church for twenty-one years. An inspired leader during a tumultuous time for Rome, he stood firm against heretics and attackers. It is believed that he met with Attila the Hun at the city gates and convinced him to leave the city in peace. He is also credited with deeming the doctrine of the Incarnation as an article of faith. A wise and beloved pontiff, St. Leo the Great died on November 10, 461.

No one, however weak, is denied a share in the victory of the cross. No one is beyond the help of the prayer of Christ.

—*St. Leo the Great*

The tempter, ever on the watch, wages war most violently against those whom he sees most careful to avoid sin.

—*St. Leo the Great*

SAINT MARTIN OF TOURS

(c. 315–397) Bishop. Born the son of a Roman soldier in the province of Pannonia, St. Martin likewise pursued a military career but experienced a dramatic vision of Christ that prompted him to embrace Christianity and seek a religious life. Ordained as an exorcist, he also spent time living as a hermit, suffered great pains for defending the faith yet adamantly opposed the death penalty for heretics. He was named bishop of Tours, established the famous monastery, and became known as one of the founders of monasticism in the region. This humble and virtuous saint died peacefully in his old age.

Lord, if your people still have need of my services, I will not avoid the toil. Your will be done. I have fought the good fight long enough. Yet if you bid me continue to hold the battle line in defense of your camp, I will never beg to be excused from failing strength. I will do the work you entrust to me. While you command, I will fight beneath your banner.

—*St. Martin of Tours*

· · · · · · · · · · · · · ·

NOVEMBER 12

SAINT JOSAPHAT

(c. 1580–1623) Eastern Rite Bishop, martyr. Born Joseph Kunsevich in a region of Poland to a noble family, he joined the Order of St. Basil as a twenty year old, took the name of Josaphat, and embarked on much needed reforms to the order. He was ordained a priest and became known as a gifted preacher. He was made bishop of Vitebsk in 1617. As bishop, he preached and tirelessly advocated to unite the Orthodox Church with Rome. The schism between the between the Eastern Church, based in Constantinople, and the Western Church of Rome dated back for centuries. Through his fiery preaching, St. Josaphat was able to win support for the union with Rome, but he was later killed by an Orthodox fanatic. St. Josaphat was canonized by Pope Innocent XI in 1867, the first saint of the Eastern Church to be canonized by Rome.

The time will come when there will be one flock and one shepherd, one faith and one clear knowledge of God.

—*St. Bridget of Sweden*

· · · · · · · · · · · · · ·

NOVEMBER 13

SAINT FRANCES XAVIER CABRINI

(1850–1917) Founder. The youngest of thirteen children born to a farming family in Northern Italy, she was drawn to the religious life as a teenager but was rejected by two communities due to her frail health. Undaunted, she devoted herself to caring for her parents and working on the family farm. At the request of the bishop, she began teaching at a girls' school and continued for six years. Still longing for a religious life, she was finally granted permission to establish the Order of Missionary Sisters of the Sacred Heart in 1880. After an audience with Pope Leo XIII, it was decided that she would travel to New York to aid the Italian immigrant population. Mother Cabrini traveled to the slums of New York City and began ministering to the sick and orphans. With the help of benefactors and the Church, Mother Cabrini soon founded schools, hospitals, and orphanages in her adopted homeland. In 1907, she became a naturalized U.S. citizen. She kept a daunting schedule until the end of her life; she collapsed in 1916 while wrapping Christmas presents for needy children in Chicago and died the following day. By the time of her death, her order had spread around the world. Canonized in 1946 by Pope Pius XII, Mother Cabrini was the first American citizen to be proclaimed a saint; she was declared the Patroness of Immigrants in 1950.

I travel, work, suffer my weak health, meet with a thousand difficulties, but all these are nothing, for this world is so small. To me, space is an imperceptible object, as I am accustomed to dwell in eternity.

—*St. Frances Xavier Cabrini*

We must pray without tiring, for the salvation of mankind does not depend on material success; nor on sciences that cloud the intellect. Neither does it depend on arms and human industries, but on Jesus alone.

—*St. Frances Xavier Cabrini*

....

NOVEMBER 14

SAINT LAWRENCE O'TOOLE

(1128–1180) Bishop. Born the child of an Irish chieftain, St. Lawrence was kidnapped at the age of ten during a raid by the king of Leinster who treated the boy miserably. The future saint's father was finally able to procure his release to the Bishop of Glendalough. St. Lawrence went on to become a monk, then an abbot, then the archbishop of Dublin. A key figure of his time, he worked ceaselessly to broker peace between England and Ireland. Famous for his piety, kindness, and charity, he invited homeless people to dine with him each evening. St. Lawrence was canonized in 1225 by Pope Honorius III.

Alas, you poor, foolish people, what will you do now? Who will take care of you in your trouble? Who will help you?

—last words of St. Lawrence, about his flock in Dublin

SAINT ALBERT THE GREAT

(1206–1280) Bishop and Doctor of the Church. Born to a noble family in Swabia, Germany, he studied at the University of Padua in Italy and found himself drawn to a religious life. He joined the Dominicans despite his family's strenuous protestations, and grew into a brilliant thinker and esteemed teacher. He studied and taught philosophy at Cologne and theology in Paris, and famously taught St. Thomas Aquinas. A prolific writer, he wrote on subjects ranging from theology and philosophy to astronomy, biology, botany, chemistry, economics, ethics, geology, and politics. In 1256, he became a papal theologian in Rome and continued to write, preach, and grow in sanctity until his peaceful death in 1280. He was proclaimed a saint and Doctor of the Church in 1931 by Pope Pius XI.

The greater and more persistent your confidence in God, the more abundantly you will receive all that you ask.

—St. Albert the Great

I shall not conceal a science that was before me revealed by the grace of God; I shall not keep it to myself, for being afraid of attracting its curse. What worth is a concealed science; what worth is a hidden treasure? The science I have learned without fiction I transmit with no regret.

—St. Albert the Great

SAINT MARGARET OF SCOTLAND

(c. 1046–1093) An English princess, St. Margaret was born and educated in Hungary while her father, King Edward the Atheling, was in exile. She and her family returned to England in 1057 and her brother briefly reigned as an uncrowned king. She and her mother later fled to Scotland when a Norman king was crowned in England in 1066. In 1070, she married King Malcolm III. St. Margaret was a devoted wife and mother of eight children, a caring queen, and a devout Christian. She did much to promote the faith, founded several churches, and spent a portion of every day in prayer and practicing austere penance. St. Margaret died only days after learning that her husband and eldest son had died in battle against the English. Venerated by the Scottish upon her death, St. Margaret was canonized in 1250 by Pope Innocent IV and named Patroness of Scotland in 1673.

When {Margaret} spoke, her conversation was with the salt of wisdom. When she was silent, her silence was filled with good thoughts. So thoroughly did her outward bearing correspond with the staidness of her character that it seemed as if she has been born the pattern of a virtuous life.

—*Turgot, Bishop of St. Andrews, St. Margaret's confessor and biographer*

SAINT ELIZABETH OF HUNGARY

(1207–1231) The daughter of King Andrew II of Hungary, she married Louis of Thuringia in 1221 and bore three children. After the death of her husband, she was forced out of the castle by her brother-in-law. She joined the Franciscan tertiaries and devoted the remainder of her life to ministering to the poor and sick. Dying at the age of twenty-four, she was canonized in 1235. St. Elizabeth is the patron of bakers.

I want to adorn myself, not out of worldly pride, but for the love of God alone—in a fitting manner, however, so as to give my husband no cause to sin, if something about me were to displease him. Only let him love me in the Lord, with a chaste, marital affection, so that we, in the same way, might hope for the reward of eternal life from Him who has sanctified the law of marriage.

—St. Elizabeth of Hungary

I heard a little bird singing. It sang so sweetly, I had to sing, too.

—St. Elizabeth, on her deathbed

. . . .

NOVEMBER 18

SAINT ROSE PHILIPPINE DUCHESNE

(1769–1852) Religious, founder. Born to a large French family in Grenoble, St. Rose dedicated her life to God at an early age. She was educated by the nuns at the Visitation Convent and at the age of eighteen she persuaded her parents to let her join their community. Her order was disbanded during the French Revolution's Reign of Terror, but she was determined to find another path to religious life. In 1804 she had the opportunity to join the Society of the Sacred Heart. Though she strongly desired to help those in the New World, it would be thirteen years before this hope was realized. At the age of forty-nine, St. Rose traveled to the United States where she and a handful of others settled in the village of St. Charles, Missouri and established the first houses of the order, as well as a boarding school and the first free school west of the Mississippi River. When she was in her seventies, she journeyed to live among the Potawatomi Indians in the Rocky Mountains and established a school for girls there. Earning the love and admiration of the tribe, she became known as the "Woman Who Prays Always." This dynamic saint—pioneer, educator, and obedient servant of God—was beatified in 1940 and canonized by Pope John Paul II in 1988.

OPPOSITE: Saint Margaret of Scotland

We cultivate a very small field for Christ but we love it, knowing that God does not require great achievements, but a heart that holds back nothing for self.

—*St. Rose Philippine Duchesne*

Never forget that the road to Heaven is the Way of the Cross. Jesus has called us to follow Him, bearing the Cross as He did.

—*St. Rose Philippine Duchesne*

SAINT OBADIAH

(c. mid-fifth century BC) Prophet. The fourth of the Twelve Minor Prophets is the presumed writer of the shortest book of the Bible. In it, he denounces the nation of Edom for its support of the Babylonian invaders of Israel. He is believed to have sheltered a vast number of prophets from the clutches of Jezebel. The prophet is said to be buried in Samaria. The name Obadiah means "servant of the Lord."

For the day of the Lord is coming against all the nations. As you have done, it shall be done to you; your deeds shall return to you.

—*Obadiah 1:15*

SAINT BERNWARD

(died 1022) Bishop. Orphaned at a young age, he was raised by his uncle, Bishop Volkmar of Utrecht. Hearing God's call, he completed his studies and was ordained in 987. He served as imperial chaplain and was the tutor to the child who would become Emperor Otto III. He was named bishop of Hildesheim in 993 and built St. Michael's Church and monastery. In addition to his spiritual gifts, St. Bernward was a gifted artisan with a keen interest in art, architecture, and metal works. He crafted metal works himself for the cathedral, including the so-called Bernward bronze doors, cross, column, and candlesticks that can still be seen at the monastery. He lovingly led his flock for thirty years. Becoming a Benedictine later in life, he died in 1022 and was canonized by Pope Celestine III in 1193.

O Blessed St. Bernward, you who faithfully led your flock for many years and were gifted with many spiritual gifts and temporal talents, through your intercession we pray that we may use our gifts and talents to glorify the Lord always. We ask this in the name of Jesus Christ, our Lord and Savior. Amen.

. . . .

THE PRESENTATION OF MARY

This feast commemorates when St. Ann and St. Joachim took Mary to the Temple to consecrate her to the Lord as a small child as was the custom of the Jews. The feast first came to be celebrated in Jerusalem, in the East from the early Middle Ages, and celebrated in the West in the fourteenth century.

The Divine Spirit, the love itself of the Father and the Son, came corporally into Mary, and enriching her with graces above all creatures, reposed in her and made her His Spouse, the Queen of Heaven and earth.
—*St. Anselm of Canterbury*

The beauty that I saw in Our Lady was extraordinary, although I didn't make out any particular details except the form of her face in general and that her garment was of the most brilliant white, not dazzling, but soft. Our Lady seemed to me to be a very young girl.
—*St. Teresa of Avila*

······

NOVEMBER 22

SAINT CECILA

(third century) Virgin, martyr. Born the daughter of wealthy Roman parents, she was betrothed to a pagan named Valerius. A convert to Christianity, St. Cecilia had pledged herself to Christ and therefore refused to consummate her marriage, revealing to her husband that her virginity was being guarded by an angel. Moved by his wife's devotion, Valerius met with Pope Urban to discuss the matter. Afterwards, he and his brother Tiburtius were convinced to embrace Christianity. They were arrested by the Romans when their faith was discovered, and they were both martyred. Several days later, after St. Cecilia also refused to renounce her faith, soldiers came to her house to kill her. They attempted to suffocate her to no avail. They then struck her three times in the neck with a sword and left her to die. She lingered for three days before meeting her heavenly reward. Since the fourteenth century, St. Cecila has been closely associated with music and is often depicted with either an organ or a lute. She is the patron of musicians.

I know not your gods. Jesus Christ, the only Son of God is my God. Beat, tear, or burn me, and if my words offend you, cut out my tongue; every part of my body is ready when God calls for it as a sacrifice.

—*St. Theodore of Heraclea*

················

NOVEMBER 23

SAINT CLEMENT I

(died c. 99). Pope, martyr. A Roman of Jewish extraction, St. Clement was a convert of St. Peter and St. Paul. Sources vary on whether he was the third or fourth successor to St. Peter. He is the author of the First Epistle to the Corinthians which was widely disseminated in the early Church. He died a martyr's death when he was thrown from a ship with an anchor around his neck. St. Clement is the patron of mariners and stone cutters.

OPPOSITE: The Presentation of Mary

Charity unites us to God. There is nothing mean in charity, nothing arrogant. Charity knows no schism, does not rebel, does all things in concord. In charity all the elect of God have been made perfect.

—*St. Clement's First Epistle to the Corinthians*

. . . .

NOVEMBER 24

SAINT ANDREW DUNG-LAC AND COMPANIONS

(died 1839) Martyrs. It is estimated that between 130,000 and 300,000 people were martyred for their Christian faith in Vietnam between the seventeenth and twentieth centuries. The Vatican professes that the torture inflicted upon these martyrs was some of the most barbaric in the history of the Church. The one hundred seventeen martyrs in this group were proclaimed saints by Pope John Paul II on June 19, 1988. The group included bishops, priests, and lay Catholics. There were ninety-six Vietnamese people, eleven Spaniards, and ten French people. St. Andrew Dung-Lac was a Vietnamese parish priest.

I am not alone—Christ is with me.

—*St. Paul Le-Bao-Tinh, one of the Vietnamese martyrs, written from prison*

. . . .

NOVEMBER 25

SAINT CATHERINE OF ALEXANDRIA

(early fourth century) Virgin, martyr. St. Catherine was born to a wealthy pagan family in Alexandria, Egypt. Her interest in philosophy led her to Christianity. After receiving a vision, St. Catherine embraced the faith and consecrated herself to Christ. When Roman emperor Maxentius began to persecute Christians, she bravely confronted him about the truth of Christianity. Her preaching and debating moved

OPPOSITE: Saint Catherine of Alexandria

many of the emperor's own philosophers to embrace Christ—as did many soldiers and members of the emperor's family, all of whom were martyred. Refusing the emperor's hand in marriage was the final insult. St. Catherine was thrown into prison, tortured on a spiked wheel, and beheaded. Legend has it that milk rather than blood poured from her severed neck. St. Catherine of Alexandria is the patron of Christian philosophers.

The martyrs desired death, not to fly labor, but to attain their end. And why did they not fear death, from which man so naturally shrinks? Because they had vanquished the natural love of their own bodies, by divine and supernatural love.

—St. Catherine of Siena

. . . .

NOVEMBER 26

SAINT JOHN BERCHMANS

(1599–1621) Born in present day Belgium, St. John was the eldest of five children born to the family. A pious child and an altar boy, St. John spent much of his time caring for his sickly mother. In 1615 he entered the Jesuit college at Mechlin, Belgium, and later traveled to Rome to continue his studies. He died suddenly after defending the faith in a debate. St. John Berchmans was canonized in 1888 by Pope Leo XIII and is the patron of altar boys.

Our true worth does not consist in what human beings think of us. What we really are consists in what God knows us to be.

—St. John Berchmans

SAINT VIRGIL OF SALZBURG

(700–784) Bishop. Born in Ireland as Feirgil to a noble family, he was likely educated at the monastery in Iona. Leaving Ireland anywhere from 723 to 745, he settled in France for several years and then in Bavaria. He later founded a monastery at Chiemsee and became the abbot at St. Peter's at Salzburg. Possessing a great and varied intellect, St. Virgil had a number of disputes with St. Boniface who appealed to Rome for resolution. In the end, St. Virgil was vindicated.

Upon the martyrdom of St. Boniface, St. Virgil was named his successor. As bishop of Salzburg, St. Virgil built the first cathedral there, monasteries, and supervised several missionary was canonized in 1233 by Pope Gregory IX.

Our Lord has created persons for all states in life, and in all of them we see people who have achieved sanctity by fulfilling their obligations well.

—*St. Anthony Mary Claret*

SAINT CATHERINE LABOURÉ

(1806–1870) Religious. Born to a humble farming family in France, she helped to care for her widowed father and worked in her uncle's café in Paris prior to seeking a religious life. St. Catherine joined the Sisters of Charity of Saint Vincent de Paul and experienced a vast array of brilliant visions of St. Vincent de Paul and the Blessed Virgin which formed the basis of the cult of the Miraculous Medal. The Blessed Mother revealed to St. Catherine that she wanted a metal struck in her image and that great graces would be granted to the wearers. From 1831 until her death, St. Catherine led a quiet life in her community caring for the elderly and tending the poultry. Shortly before her death she was revealed as the Miraculous Medal visionary. Many people made the pilgrimage to her funeral and miraculous cures were reported at her tomb.

St. Catherine was beatified in 1933 and canonized in 1947.

One must see God in everyone.

—*St. Catherine Labouré*

O Mary, conceived without sin. Pray for us who have recourse to Thee.

—*words revealed to St. Catherine by the Blessed Mother and inscribed on the Miraculous Medal*

SAINT FRANCIS ANTHONY OF LUCERA

(1681–1742) St. Francis Anthony was born to a family of Italian farmers. He lost his father at a young age but was raised by a kind stepfather who sent him to the Franciscans for his education. Joining the order at fifteen, Brother Francis Anthony was ordained a priest in 1705 at the tomb of his spiritual father St. Francis of Assisi. He earned his doctorate of theology in Rome, taught philosophy, was a gifted preacher, and devoted himself to helping all those in need—prisoners, the poor, and the sick. St. Francis Anthony predicted his own death and met his heavenly reward in 1742. He was beatified in 1957 by Pope Pius XII and canonized by Pope John Paul II in 1986.

All this reverence that is paid to me I never take to myself, but I simply pass it all on to God.

—*St. Francis of Assisi*

SAINT ANDREW

(died c. 60) Apostle, martyr. The brother of St. Peter, St. Andrew was called by Jesus to become a follower when he saw the brothers casting nets into the Sea of Galilee. Jesus beckoned them to follow him and become "fishers of men" whereupon they dropped their nets and followed him. St. Andrew is believed to have been a disciple of St. John the Baptist. As written in the Gospel, it was St. Andrew who approached Jesus about the loaves and the fishes, asking how they were to feed the multitude with their meager supply of food (see John 6:8-9). St. Andrew was also believed present at the Last Supper. Tradition indicates that St. Andrew evangelized in the region of Greece and Turkey and even perhaps as far as Russia and Poland. He was martyred at Patras in Achaia, and, upon learning of his fate, requested to be crucified on a cross in the form of an "X" believing himself unworthy to die on a cross similar to that of Christ.

That the preaching of these men was indeed divine is clearly brought home to us when we consider how else could twelve uneducated men, who lived on lakes and rivers and wastelands, get the idea for such an immense enterprise? How could men who perhaps had never been in a city or a public forum think of setting out to do battle with the whole world?

—*...a sick beggar to rest in St. Martin's bed while he cared for the man.*

DECEMBER

DECEMBER 1

SAINT EDMUND CAMPION

(1540–1581) Priest, martyr. Born in London, the son of a Catholic printer and bookseller, St. Edmund was a bright boy who studied at the University of Oxford when he was fifteen. He grew up amid the upheaval and persecution that ensued following King Henry VIII's break with the Church. He excelled at Oxford and became a brilliant lecturer there. He most likely took the Oath of Supremacy and was ordained an Anglican deacon. In time, he came to realize that Catholicism was the true path. He journeyed to Ireland where he studied and taught for several years and then escaped to France where he reconciled with the Catholic Church. He joined the Jesuits in 1573 and was ordained a priest in 1578. Thereafter, he taught at the Jesuit college in Prague. In 1580, St. Edmund was sent on a missionary journey back to England. He entered the country using a false identity with several other priests. He immediately began visiting and ministering to Catholics in hiding. Less than a year later, he was betrayed and arrested. Thrown into the Tower of London, he was tortured, tried, and convicted of treason. He and two other priests were brutally tortured and executed. Beatified in 1886, St. Edmund was canonized by Pope Paul VI in 1970 together with thirty-nine others, all known as the Forty Martyrs of England and Wales.

In condemning us, you condemn all your own ancestors, all our ancient bishops and kings, all that was once the glory of England— the island of saints, and the most devoted child of the See of Peter.

—St. Edmund Campion, upon hearing that he had been found guilty of treason, November 20, 1581

To all those who are filled with admiration in reading the records of these martyrs, it is perfectly clear that they are worthy to stand alongside the greatest martyrs of the past; and this is not merely because of their fearless faith and marvellous constancy, but by reason of their humility, simplicity and serenity, and above all the spiritual joy and that wonderously radiant love with which they accepted their condemnation and death.

—Pope Paul VI, at the canonization of the Forty Martyrs of England and Wales, October 25, 1970

. . . .

DECEMBER 2

SAINT BIBIANA

(fourth century) Virgin and martyr. St. Bibiana was one of two daughters born to Christian parents in Rome. Under the reign of the emperor Julian the Apostate, it is believed that the saint's father, mother, and sister were killed for their Christian faith. St. Bibiana, who also clung to her faith, was the last of her family to die. She was tortured, scourged, and beaten to death by her executioner when she refused to renounce Christ. Her cult was popular in fifth century Rome.

They will expel you from the synagogues; in fact, the hour is coming when everyone who kills you will think he is offering worship to God. They will do this because they have not known either the Father or me. I have told you this so that when their hour comes you may remember that I told you.

—John 16:2–4

. . . .

DECEMBER 3

SAINT FRANCIS XAVIER

(1506–1552) Priest, missionary. This great missionary saint was born in Spain to an aristocratic family. At the age of seventeen he traveled to the University of Paris where he studied philosophy for several years. While there he met St. Ignatius of Loyola, fifteen years his senior, who had experienced his dramatic conversion while convalescing from a war injury. The two became close friends and St. Ignatius invited St. Francis to join him in forming the Society of Jesus. Though he was initially reluctant to put aside his worldly ambitions, St. Francis was finally inspired to join his friend in forming the Jesuits along with a handful of others. Ordained in 1537, Francis left shortly after for Portugal and started his life's work of spreading the Good News. In 1541, he left for India where he converted thousands to Christianity. In 1549, he became the first missionary to set foot in Japan and was surprisingly successful there. In 1552, he set sail for China. Several weeks into his journey, he came down with a fever and was brought to an island where he died at the age of forty-six. St. Francis Xavier was canonized by Pope Gregory XV on March 12, 1622, together with St. Ignatius Loyola. He is the copatron of missionaries with St. Thérèse of Lisieux.

It is not the actual physical exertion that counts towards a one's progress, nor the nature of the task, but by the spirit of faith with which it is undertaken.

—*St. Francis Xavier*

God's love calls us to move beyond fear. We ask God for the courage to abandon ourselves unreservedly, so that we might be molded by God's grace, even as we cannot see where that path may lead us.

—*St. Ignatius Loyola*

....

DECEMBER 4

SAINT BARBARA

(fourth century) Martyr. Born to a wealthy pagan family in present day Turkey, St. Barbara was locked in a tower by her tyrannical father Dioscorus when he became obsessed with secluding his beautiful daughter from society. She was somehow introduced to Christianity and secretly baptized. Legend states that Dioscorus was enraged when he learned of his daughter's conversion and that he, a loyal Roman citizen, beheaded her himself rather than accept her Christianity. It is believed that upon her death, Dioscorus was struck and killed by lightning. St. Barbara was venerated from the ninth century onward.

OPPOSITE: Saint Barbara

She is the patron of miners, military engineers, anyone who works with explosives, as well as victims of fire and lightning strikes. Unable to verify whether the saint's cult was based on legend or fact, the Church removed St. Barbara from the General Roman Calendar in 1969, but she is still venerated by the faithful—both in the Catholic Church and in the Eastern Orthodox Church—all over the world.

O God, Who did adorn Your holy Virgin and Martyr Barbara with extraordinary fortitude in the confession of the Faith, and did console her in the most atrocious torments; grant us through her intercession perseverance in the fulfillment of Your law and the grace of being fortified before our end with the holy Sacraments, and of a happy death. Through Christ our Lord. Amen.

—Prayer in honor of St. Barbara

. . . .

DECEMBER 5

SAINT CRISPINA

(died 304). Martyr. Born in present day Tunisia, St. Crispina was a wife and mother of a prominent family living in North Africa during the reign of Diocletian. As was the practice during the persecutions, she was ordered to make a sacrifice to the gods. When she refused, she was tried but proved steadfast in her faith. Publicly humiliated and mocked, she was then beheaded. The facts of her martyrdom are revealed in the notes from her trial which are still in existence. St. Crispina was honored for her martyrdom in the days of St. Augustine, who mentioned St. Crispina and her holiness in many of his sermons.

My God who is and who abides forever ordered me to be born; it was He who gave me salvation through the saving waters of baptism. He is at my side, helping me, strengthening His hand-maid in all things so that I will not commit sacrilege.

—St. Crispina, from her trial

SAINT NICHOLAS OF MYRA

(died c. 342) Bishop. St. Nicholas was a native of Asia Minor, born to wealthy parents. An exceptionally pious child, he was raised by an uncle after his parents died in a plague. Drawn to religious life, he joined a monastery in the Holy Land in or about 305. In 317, he felt called back to his homeland and was later named the bishop of Myra. Famously devoted to performing acts of charity, he once secretly deposited a bag of gold on three different occasions to a family who had no money for the dowry of their daughters. It was this episode that evolved into the tradition of gift-giving on the saint's feast. The beloved saint died in Myra and had many churches dedicated in his honor. He is the special patron of children and sailors and is venerated by Christian faithful throughout the world.

The giver of every good and perfect gift has called upon us to mimic God's giving, by grace, through faith, and this is not of ourselves.

—St. Nicholas of Myra

. . . .

DECEMBER 7

SAINT AMBROSE

(340–397) Bishop and Doctor of the Church. The son of the Roman prefect of Gaul, St. Ambrose finished his studies and embarked on a career in law and politics. Moving to Milan, he was appointed the governor of Liguria and Aemilia. When the See of Milan became vacant, the disputing Catholics and Arians joined forces to unanimously elect St. Ambrose as their bishop. Not yet baptized, St. Ambrose was baptized, made deacon, ordained priest, and consecrated bishop all in a week's time. St. Ambrose vigorously defended the faith against the Arian and other prevalent heresies. He was the first of the Desert Fathers and Doctors of the Church to address church-state interactions and did much to clarify and define the Church's role in its own domain. St. Ambrose was instrumental in achieving the conversion of St. Augustine and had the privilege of baptizing the great saint. After a lifetime of service to the Lord and his flock, St. Ambrose died a peaceful death in 397. He is the patron of Milan.

Patient endurance is the perfection of charity.

—St. Ambrose

The soul is the user, the body for use; hence the one is master, the other servant.

—St. Ambrose

THE IMMACULATE CONCEPTION OF THE BLESSED VIRGIN MARY

This feast celebrates that the Blessed Mother was conceived in the womb of her mother, St. Ann, without original sin. First celebrated in the seventh century by the Eastern Church, the feast was originally honored in the West in the eighth century. It was renamed the Immaculate Conception in the eleventh century, and the Immaculate Conception was declared as dogma by Pope Pius IX on December 8, 1854.

We declare, pronounce and define that the doctrine which holds that the Blessed Virgin Mary, at the first instant of her conception, by a singular privilege and grace of the Omnipotent God, in virtue of the merits of Jesus Christ, the Savior of mankind, was preserved immaculate from all stain of original sin, has been revealed by God, and therefore should firmly and constantly be believed by all the faithful. . . .

—Pope Pius IX, *proclaiming the dogma of the Immaculate Conception of the Blessed Virgin Mary, December 8, 1854*

He chose her from the beginning, from the very first moment of conception, making her worthy of the divine motherhood to which she would be called at the appointed time. He made her the first heir to

OPPOSITE: Saint Nicholas of Myra

the holiness of her own Son. The first among those redeemed by his blood, which he had received from her, humanly speaking. He made her spotless at the very moment of conception.

—Pope John Paul II, from his homily on the Feast of the Immaculate Conception, December 8, 1978

DECEMBER 9

SAINT JUAN DIEGO

(1474–1548) Visionary, hermit, catechist. Given the name Cuauhtlatoatzin ("The eagle who speaks") at his birth, St. Juan was a member of the Chichimeca people who was among the early converts to Christianity. He was a fifty-seven year old widower, walking the several miles it took to get to Mass one day, when the Blessed Mother appeared to him, the first of four apparitions. After the apparitions it is believed that St. Juan retired to live as a hermit in a hut near the first chapel built to honor Our Lady of Guadalupe. He spent the rest of his days in prayer, penance, and meeting with pilgrims who journeyed to the shrine of Our Lady. St. Juan was beatified in 1990 and canonized in 2002 by Pope John Paul II.

Hear and let it penetrate into your heart, my dear little son: let nothing discourage you, nothing depress you. Let nothing alter your heart or your countenance. Also, do not fear any illness or vexation, anxiety or pain. Am I not here who am your mother? Are you not under my shadow and protection? Am I not your fountain of life? Are you not in the folds of my mantle, in the crossing of my arms? Is there anything else that you need?

—Our Lady of Guadalupe's words to St. Juan Diego

In accepting the Christian message without forgoing his indigenous identity, Juan Diego discovered the profound truth of the new

OPPOSITE: The Immaculate Conception of the Blessed Virgin Mary

humanity, in which we are all called to be children of God. Thus he facilitated the fruitful meeting of two worlds and became the catalyst for the new Mexican identity, closely united to Our Lady of Guadalupe, whose mestizo face expresses her spiritual motherhood, which embraces all Mexicans.

—Pope John Paul II, from his canonization homily of St. Juan Diego

. . . .
DECEMBER 10

SAINT GREGORY III

(died 741) Pope. Born of Syrian heritage, St. Gregory III was elected pope by popular acclamation while he was at the funeral of his predecessor, Pope Gregory II. During his papacy, he faced the Iconoclast Controversy, which had begun during the papacy of Pope Gregory II. St. Gregory III stood firm against the Iconoclasts and supported the use of religious images or icons for Christians, which had been the tradition among Christians dating back to the beginning of the second century. St. Gregory III has the distinction of being the last non-European pope until Pope Francis was elected pope in 2013.

Keep your eyes on the crucifix; for Jesus without the cross is a man without a mission, and the cross without Jesus is a burden without a reliever.

—Archbishop Fulton J. Sheen

Let the crucifix be not only in my eyes and on my breast, but in my heart.

—St. Bernadette Soubirous

OPPOSITE: Saint Juan Diego

SAINT DAMASUS I

(c. 306–385) Pope. A humble priest in Rome, St. Damasus was sixty years old when he was elected pope in 366, the successor of Pope Liberius. He immediately encountered controversy when a rival vied for the papacy, though St. Damasus was soon accepted as the legitimate pope. He is known for asserting the primacy of Rome, assiduously defending the faith against heresy, and for promoting the veneration of martyrs. He was beloved by St. Jerome who served as the papal secretary for the last several years of the pontificate. Known for his great humility, love of the poor, and his holiness, St. Damasus died at the age of seventy-nine after leading the Church for more than eighteen years.

An incomparable person, learned in the Scriptures, a virgin doctor of the virgin Church, who loved chastity and heard its praises with pleasure.

—St. Jerome describing St. Damasus I

OUR LADY OF GUADALUPE

This feast dates back to the sixteenth century and commemorates the appearances of the Blessed Virgin to Juan Diego, an Aztec convert, near Mexico City beginning on December 9, 1531. She asked that a church be built on the spot where she appeared. For evidence of her presence, she sent Juan Diego to the bishop with an abundance of roses that had miraculously bloomed in the winter, and the imprint of her likeness on his cloak. It is estimated that millions of Native Americans converted to Christianity after the appearance of Our Lady at Guadalupe. The cloak, known as a "tilma," is still displayed at the Basilica of Our Lady of Guadalupe in Mexico City. The shrine of Our Lady of Guadalupe is one of the most visited sites for pilgrimage in all of North America and many miracles have been received through the intercession of Mary under this title. Our Lady of Guadalupe is the Patroness of Mexico and the Patroness of the Unborn.

Our Lady of Guadalupe, mystical rose, make intercession for our Holy Church, protect the Sovereign Pontiff, help all those who invoke you in their necessities, and since you are the ever Virgin Mary and Mother of God, obtain for us from your most holy Son the grace of keeping our faith, hope in the midst of the bitterness of life, burning love and the precious gift of final perseverance. Amen.

—*Prayer to Our Lady of Guadalupe*

DECEMBER 13

SAINT LUCY

(c. 283–c. 304) Born in Syracuse, Sicily to wealthy nobles, she was a devout Christian who consecrated herself to Christ as a girl and took a vow of chastity. When she gave her wealth and possessions away to the poor, a suitor who felt spurned turned her in to the authorities as a Christian. Refusing to renounce her faith, she was imprisoned and tortured. Legend has it that St. Lucy plucked her eyes out and sent them to her suitor, as he had always loved her eyes. Her vision was believed to be miraculously restored the following day. She finally met her end when she was stabbed by a dagger in the neck. St. Lucy is the patron saint of the poor, eyes, and diseases of the eye.

Relying on Your goodness, O God, we humbly ask you, by the intercession of your servant, St. Lucy, to give perfect vision to our eyes, that we may serve for your greater honor and glory. And we pray for the salvation of our souls in this world, that we may come to the enjoyment of the unfailing light of the Lamb of God in heaven. St. Lucy, virgin and martyr, hear our prayers and answer our petitions. Amen.

—*Prayer in honor of St. Lucy*

SAINT JOHN OF THE CROSS

(1542–1591) Priest and Doctor of the Church. St. John was born Juan de Yepes to a poor family in Spain. His father died suddenly after contracting a fever, and his mother was left to raise three young children with the meager money she earned as weaver. A compassionate priest helped the family and after St. John's rowdy brother had a dramatic spiritual conversion, St. John began to realize his own spiritual calling. He studied at the Jesuit college, and at the age of twenty-one, joined the Carmelite Order, inspired by his special devotion to the Blessed Mother. He was ordained a priest when he was twenty-five. Desiring a more contemplative spiritual path, St. John was considering a move to a different religious community when his friend St. Teresa of Avila challenged him to join her in reforming the order. He thus went on to co-found Discalced Carmelite friars with St. Teresa. He suffered tremendously and faced great persecution in achieving the reform of the order—including being kidnapped and imprisoned for nine months by monks who felt his reforms were destructive. St. John continued to battle hostile members of his order and finally succumbed to illness in 1591 at the age of forty-nine. A towering mystic, poet, and spiritual writer, he was canonized in 1726 and made Doctor of the Church by Pope Pius XI in 1926.

The more lofty the degree of loving union to which God destines the soul, so much more profound and persistent must be its purification.

—*St. John of the Cross*

The virtuous soul that is alone and without a master, is like a lone burning coal; it will grow colder rather than hotter. Those who fall alone remain alone in their fall, and they value their souls little since they entrust it to themselves alone. If you do not fear falling alone, do you presume that you will rise up alone? Consider how much more can be accomplished by two together than by one alone.

—*St. John of the Cross*

And when I spoke with this young friar, he pleased me very much. I learned from him how he also wanted to go to the Carthusians. Telling him what I was attempting to do, I begged him to wait until the Lord would give us a monastery and pointed out the great good that would be accomplished if in his desire to improve he were to remain in his own order and that much greater service would be rendered to the Lord. He promised me he would remain as long as he wouldn't have to wait long.

—*St. Teresa of Avila, about her first meeting with St. John of the Cross*

. . . .
DECEMBER 15

SAINT MARY DI ROSA

(1813–1855) Religious, founder. This saint was born Paola Francesca di Rosa into a large wealthy family in Brescia, Italy. St. Mary was a happy and devout child who was educated by nuns. At the age of seventeen, she lost her mother and dedicated herself to helping raise her siblings and to assisting her father with his business. Greatly desiring the religious life, she began working with young girls in need, and helping the sick, especially during the cholera outbreak of 1836. She finally realized her dream when she founded the Handmaids of Charity devoted to caring for the sick in hospitals, on battlefields, and working in schools and orphanages. Taking the name Mary Crucified (Mary Crucifixa), she faithfully led her order until her death. St. Mary di Rosa was canonized in 1954.

Charity begins today. Today somebody is suffering, today somebody is in the street, today somebody is hungry. Our work is for today, yesterday has gone, tomorrow has not yet come. We have only today to make Jesus known, loved, served, fed, clothed, sheltered. Tomorrow we will not have the if we do not feed them today.

—*Blessed Teresa of Calcutta*

SAINT ADELAIDE OF BURGANDY

(931–999) Empress. Born to a noble family of Burgandy, St. Adelaide was married for several years to the depraved King Lothair II of Italy. As a young widow, she was harangued by the king's successor, but she finally found a loving husband in Otto I of Germany. In 962 she was named empress of the Holy Roman Empire, and she and Otto reigned for twenty years. Always devoted to works of charity and kindness, she retreated to a convent of her founding upon her husband's death and spent the remainder of her life focused on prayer. Upon her death, she was venerated as a saint and canonized in 1097.

The state of marriage is one that requires more virtue and constancy than any other. It is a perpetual exercise in mortification.

—*St. Francis de Sales*

SAINT HILDEGARD OF BINGEN

(1098–1179) Visionary, Doctor of the Church. Born to a large, noble family, St. Hildegard was a frail child who was graced with spiritual visions before the age of five. Her family sent her to live with a holy woman known as Blessed Jutta who became her teacher and spiritual director for ten years. When St. Hildegard was eighteen, she became a Benedictine nun at the monastery where Jutta was abbess. When Blessed Jutta died, it was unanimously decided that St. Hildegard be named abbess. At the instruction of her confessor, she began to write about the dazzling visions she'd been receiving all of her life. In addition to her spiritual works, she also penned thousands of letters to those seeking her counsel. She faced her share of controversy and was even excommunicated for a time along with her entire convent for permitting the burial of an excommunicated noble woman. Still, she was consulted by kings, popes, saints, and leaders for her sage advice. Though she was venerated locally and considered a saint by the Church of England, it was not until May 2012 that Pope Benedict XVI declared this holy woman a saint. She was named a Doctor of the Church in October 2012.

Man, too, is God's handiwork, like every other creature. But man is also God's journeyman and the foreshadowing of the mysteries of God.

—*St. Hildegard of Bingen*

Now observe the sun and the moon and stars and all the decoration of the greenness of the earth and consider how much prosperity God gives man with these things, although man sits with great temerity against God. . . . Who gives you a part in these bright and good things, if not God?

—*St. Hildegard of Bingen*

....

DECEMBER 18

SAINT GATIAN

(late third century) Bishop. A companion of St. Dionysius, St. Gatian evangelized at Tours in Gaul, and was the first bishop of Tours. Surrounded by pagans, he persisted in his efforts to spread the Good News and gained many converts. He continued his labors for more than fifty years until he died a peaceful death.

I must preach so that the most illiterate laborer can understand me.

—*St. Alphonsus Ligouri*

....

DECEMBER 19

BLESSED URBAN V

(born c. 1310) Pope. Born in Grisac, France, to a noble family, Blessed Urban joined the Benedictines, was ordained a priest, and studied at the top universities in Europe. He later taught law at Avignon, and became the abbot of several monasteries. Elected pope in 1362, he was the successor of Pope Innocent VI. He was crowned at Avignon, as this was during the 170 year period when the papacy was seated in Avignon. Despite being elected pope, he continued to adhere to the Benedictine Rule and opted for a humble lifestyle and attire. During his papacy, he introduced many reforms and established numerous universities and colleges. In 1367, he did attempt to return the papacy to Rome. He journeyed back to Rome and began the monumental task of rebuilding and restoring the basilicas and papal buildings that had fallen into disrepair; he likewise offered jobs to the poor and set out to bring discipline back to the clergy. Despite all of his best efforts, he was forced back to France in 1370 after the outbreak of war, and he died several months later. Blessed Urban V was beatified by Pope Pius IX in 1870.

Only the Church of Peter, to whose lot fell Italy when the disciples were sent out to preach, has always stood fast in the faith. While the faith has disappeared or has partly decayed in other regions, the Church of Peter still flourishes in faith and free from heresy.

—*St. Thomas Aquinas*

. . . .

DECEMBER 20

SAINT DOMINIC OF SILOS

(eleventh century) Abbot. Born in the Spanish province La Rioja, St. Dominic was a devout child who labored as a shepherd in the mountains of Spain. Drawn to a religious life, St. Dominic joined the Benedictines of San Milan de la Cogolla where he was eventually named the abbot. When he refused to give monastery land to the king of Navarre, he was forced to leave his monastery. He found refuge with King Ferdinand I of Old Castille who gave him a run-down monastery of St. Sebastian at Silos. St. Dominic was successful in restoring the monastery in a short time back to a thriving community. Known for his piety and miraculous healing, St. Dominic is the protector of women in labor and it is believed that through his intercession the mother of the other St. Dominic— founder of the Dominicans—was aided in her difficult pregnancy and named her child after St. Dominic of Silos.

Nothing seems tiresome or painful when you are working for a Master who pays well; who rewards even a cup of cold water given for love of Him.

—St. Dominic of Silos

DECEMBER 21

SAINT PETER CANISIUS

(1521–1597) Priest and Doctor of the Church. Born in present day Netherlands, St. Peter was trained as a lawyer but felt drawn to the Society of Jesus after hearing the inspired preaching of the early Jesuits. He joined the Society of Jesus in 1543 and was later ordained a priest. He became a leading voice of the Counter-Reformation, vigorously defending and helping to restore the faith throughout Germany, Austria, Bohemia, Moravia, and Switzerland. A prolific theologian, he wrote an enormously popular catechism called *Summary of Christian Doctrine* along with two smaller catechisms that were translated into fifteen languages and went through more than two hundred printings. Known as the Second Apostle of Germany after St. Boniface. St. Peter Canisius was canonized by Pope Pius XI in 1925 and named a Doctor of the Church.

See, O merciful God, what return
I, Your thankless servant, have made
for the innumerable favors
and the wonderful love You have shown me!
What wrongs I have done, what good left undone!
Wash away, I beg You, these faults and stains
with Your precious blood, most kind Redeemer,
and make up for my poverty by applying Your merits.
Give me the protection I need to amend my life.
I give and surrender myself wholly to You,
and offer You all I possess,

with the prayer that You bestow Your grace on me,
so that I may be able to devote and employ
all the thinking power of my mind
and the strength of my body in Your holy service,
who are God blessed for ever and ever. Amen.

—*Prayer of St. Peter Canisius*

. . . .

DECEMBER 22

SAINT CHAEREMON AND COMPANIONS

(died c. 250) Martyrs. St. Chaeremon was the Bishop of Nilopolis in Egypt. When the fierce persecutions of Christians erupted under Emperor Trajanus Decius, the holy man fled into the desert along with many other Christians. St. Chaeremon was said to have hidden in the mountains with a companion and was never heard from again. St. Chaeremon's name is listed in the Roman Martyrology for this date.

You, if you are an apostle, will not have to die. You will move to a new house: that is all.

—*Venerable José*

. . . .

DECEMBER 23

SAINT JOHN OF KANTI

(c. 1390– c. 1473) Born in Kanti, Poland to a wealthy landowning family, St. John studied at the University of Krakow. Feeling drawn to a religious life, St. John was ordained in 1424. He spent some time as a parish priest but most of his religious life was devoted to teaching theology and philosophy at the University of Krakow. He strongly desired to achieve martyrdom and made a pilgrimage to Jerusalem where he preached especially to the Turkish inhabitants there. He journeyed four times to Rome on foot and practiced measures of extreme austerity such as sleeping on the floor and the permanent abstinence from meat—all to increase in virtue.

His last act of charity was to distribute all of his worldly possessions to the poor. This devoted saint died in on Christmas Eve in 1474 and was canonized by Pope Clement XIII in 1767. He is the patron of Poland and Lithuania.

Guard against causing trouble and slandering others, for it is difficult to right the evil done.
　　　　—St. John of Kanti, his inscription on the wall of his room, following the example
　　　　　　　　　　　　of St. Augustine, to protect himself from the temptation of gossip

. . . .

DECEMBER 24

SAINT CHARBEL OR SHARBEL

(1828–1898) Born Youssef Makhlouf in Northern Lebanon, he felt drawn to live a hermit's life for God and at the age of twenty-three he joined the Monastery of St. Maroun and was later ordained to the priesthood. Deeply desirous of living a solitary life of prayer, St. Charbel had to wait seven years before he was allowed to do so. For the last twenty-three years of his life, he lived as a hermit practicing severe penance such as wearing a hair shirt, sleeping on a mattress of straw with a board for a pillow, and ate only one meager meal a day. He died on Christmas Eve of 1898. Months after his death his body was found to be incorrupt but releasing a strange red goo-like liquid. More than twenty years later, his body was again exhumed and the strange reddish liquid was still being released from his pores. In 1976, the body was again exhumed and only the skeletal remains were present, though it was said the bones bore a red hue. St. Charbel was beatified by Pope Paul VI in 1965 and canonized in 1977.

A hermit of Mount Lebanon is enrolled in the number of the blessed . . . a new eminent member of monastic sanctity has by his example and his intercession enriched the entire Christian people . . . may he make us understand, in a world largely fascinated by wealth and comfort, the paramount value of poverty, penance and asceticism, to liberate the soul in its ascent to God.
　　　　　　　　　　　　　　—Pope Paul VI, at the beatification of St. Charbel

THE NATIVITY OF OUR LORD AND SAVIOR JESUS CHRIST

The birth of Jesus Christ has been celebrated on December 25 since the mid 300's which was during the papacy of Pope Liberius. The date of December 25 had been the date of a well known pagan festival celebrated in connection with the winter solstice. The devotion to the infant Christ child was also greatly increased by St. Francis of Assisi in 1223 when he displayed the first Nativity scene, being inspired to do so after a journey to the Holy Land.

For this day in the city of David there has been born to you a Savior who is Christ, the Lord.

—Luke 2:11

Christ is the Morning Star,
who, when the night of this world is past,
gives to his saints the promise of the light of life,
and opens everlasting day.

—St. Bede the Venerable

God rescued us from the power of darkness and brought us into the kingdom of his beloved Son. Through him we have redemption, the forgiveness of our sins. He is the image of the invisible God, the first-born of all creatures.

—Colossians, 1:13-15

Every day, Jesus humbles Himself just as He did when He came from His heavenly throne into the Virgin's womb; every day He comes to us and lets us see Him in abjection, when He descends from the bosom of the Father into the hands of the priest at the altar.

—St. Francis of Assisi

OPPOSITE: The Nativity of our Lord and Savior Jesus Christ

SAINT STEPHEN

(died c. 35) Martyr. A disciple of Christ, probably of Greek and Jewish heritage, St. Stephen was one of the seven deacons chosen after the Ascension to help care for all of the new converts to Christianity. The deacons were responsible for justly distributing alms, especially to widows. As written in the Acts of the Apostles, "Stephen was full of grace and power did great wonders and signs among the people." Falsely accused of blasphemy against Moses and God, St. Stephen was dragged before the Sanhedrin, condemned to be sent out of the city and stoned to death. He died proclaiming his forgiveness for his accusers and murderers.

Look, I see the heavens opened and the Son of Man standing at the right hand of God! Lord, Jesus, receive my spirit. Lord, do not hold this sin against them.

—St. Stephen, at his death

SAINT JOHN THE APOSTLE

(died c. 100) Apostle. Born in Bethsaida, Judea, St. John was the son of Zebedee and the brother of St. James. The brothers were fisherman that Jesus summoned to follow him. The brothers were called "Sons of Thunder" by Jesus. Referred to as "the disciple whom Jesus loved," St. John had a singular relationship with Jesus; he reclined next to Jesus at the Last Supper; he was the only Apostle to stay at the foot of the cross during the crucifixion. Jesus told John from the cross to take Mary into his care after his death, and told his mother to look upon John as her son. St. John is the author of the Gospel according to John, three Epistles, and is the likely author of the Book of Revelation. It is believed that St. John preached in Asia Minor, founded many churches there, and was the last Apostle to die—dying a natural death at the age of ninety-four. St. John is the patron of booksellers, theologians, writers, and all those who work in the production of books.

In the beginning was the Word, and the Word was with God, and the Word was God. He was in the beginning with God. All things came to be through him, and without him nothing came to be. What came to be through him was life, and this life was the light of the human race; the light shines in the darkness, and the darkness has not overcome it.

—John 1:1–5

. . . .

HOLY INNOCENTS

(date unknown) Martyrs. This feast commemorates the murder of the children of Bethlehem two years and younger by King Herod. Hearing from the Magi about the birth of a king, Herod ordered the children slaughtered as a means of protecting his power. The feast of the Holy Innocents was observed as far back as the first century.

Blessed are you, Bethlehem in the land of Judah! You suffered the inhumanity of King Herod in the murder of your babes and thereby have become worthy to offer to the Lord a pure host of infants. In full right do we celebrate the heavenly birthday of these children whom the world caused to be born unto an eternally blessed life rather than that from their mothers' womb, for they attained the grace of everlasting life before the enjoyment of the present. The precious death of any martyr deserves high praise because of his heroic confession; the death of these children is precious in the sight of God because of the beatitude they gained so quickly. For already at the beginning of their lives they pass on. The end of the present life is for them the beginning of glory. These then, whom Herod's cruelty tore as sucklings from their mothers' bosom, are justly hailed as "infant martyr flowers"; they were the Church's first blossoms, matured by the frost of persecution during the cold winter of unbelief.

—St. Augustine of Hippo

DECEMBER 29

SAINT THOMAS BECKET

(c. 1117) Bishop, martyr. Born in London, St. Thomas studied theology and ecclesiastic law and was a colleague of the bishop of Canterbury. He became a close friend of King Henry II who appointed him to the position of archbishop of Canterbury while he was already serving as the chancellor of England. As St. Thomas grew increasingly spiritual, his relationship with the king grew increasingly strained. At one point, St. Thomas fled to France for seven years to escape Henry's wrath. Upon returning to England, St. Thomas again vexed the king, this time by refusing to rescind the censure on some of the king's favored bishops, thus prompting the king to declare, "Will no one rid me of this troublesome priest?" Taking his plea literally, four knights killed the saint as he was praying in Canterbury Cathedral on December 29, 1170. The murder shocked civilized people everywhere and within three years of his death, St. Thomas Becket was canonized by Pope Alexander III.

There are a great many bishops in the Church, but would to God we were the zealous teachers and pastors that we promised to be at our consecration, and still make profession of being. The harvest is good and one reaper or even several would not suffice to gather all of it into the granary of the Lord. Yet the Roman Church remains the head of all the churches and the source of Catholic teaching. Of this there can be no doubt. Everyone knows that the keys of the kingdom of heaven were given to Peter. Upon his faith and teaching the whole fabric of the Church will continue to be built until we all reach full maturity in Christ and attain to unity in faith and knowledge of the Son of God.

—St. Thomas Becket

I accept death for the name of Jesus and for the Church.

—St. Thomas Becket, his last words

SAINT FELIX I

(died 274) Pope. Born to a Roman family, St. Felix was the successor to Pope Dionysius and led the Church from 269 to 274. It is believed he was the first pope to sanction the ancient custom of celebrating mass on the anniversary of a martyr's death at his or her grave. A staunch defender of the faith, he upheld the findings of the Synod of Antioch who had deposed Paul of Samostata, the bishop of Antioch, who denied the divinity of Christ. It is unclear whether St. Felix died a natural death or was martyred during the persecution of Aurelian, but he is said to have died in 274.

Bless the martyrs heartily, that you may be a martyr by intention. Thus, even though you depart this life without persecutor, fire, or lash, you will still be found worthy of the same reward.

—St. Basil the Great

SAINT SYLVESTER I

(died 335) Pope. Born in Rome, St. Sylvester I was ordained in Rome and he became the first pope after Constantine the Great enacted the Edict of Milan which allowed Christians some measure of freedom to worship. Faithfully leading the Church for twenty-one years, he is credited with the founding of important churches in Rome and expanding the influence of the Church during his papacy. A staunch defender of the faith, he assembled the famous Council of Nicea which condemned the Arian heresy.

Do not defile yourselves with the Arians, for that teaching is not from the apostles, but from the demons, and from their father, the devil; Indeed, it is infertile, irrational, and incorrect in understanding, like the senselessness of mules.

—St. Anthony of Egypt

NEXT PAGE: Saint Sylvester I

SILVESTER PAPA